JUMP SOUL

JUMP SOUL

Charlie Smith

NEW AND SELECTED POEMS

W. W. NORTON & COMPANY

New York · London

For information about permission to reproduce selections from this book, write to
Permissions, W. W. Norton & Company, Inc., 500 Fifth Avenue, New York, NY 10110

For information about special discounts for bulk purchases, please contact
W. W. Norton Special Sales at specialsales@wwnorton.com or 800-233-4830

Manufacturing by Courier Westford
Production manager: Anna Oler

Library of Congress Cataloging-in-Publication Data

Smith, Charlie, 1947–
[Poems. Selections]
Jump soul : new and selected poems / Charlie Smith. — First Edition.
     pages cm
Includes index.
ISBN 978-0-393-24022-1 (hardcover)
I. Title.
PS3569.M5163A6 2014
811'.54—dc23

2013044103

W. W. Norton & Company, Inc.
500 Fifth Avenue, New York, N.Y. 10110
www.wwnorton.com

W. W. Norton & Company Ltd.
Castle House, 75/76 Wells Street, London W1T 3QT

1 2 3 4 5 6 7 8 9 0

Contents

GODZILLA STREET: NEW POEMS

1. JANE STREET

SELECTED POEMS

from WORD COMIX

Acknowledgments

The New Republic, Poetry, The Paris Review, Tin House, Ploughshares, Crazyhorse, Virginia Quarterly Review, Pleiades, Margie, Narrative, Big City Lit, Phoenix, Plume, Men in Miami Hotels, and *The Same*

GODZILLA STREET

NEW POEMS

I. JANE STREET

Jump Soul

. . . spirit like an aviary in one of the old zoos—
nets, gym-high ceiling—when an off-handed clap, scutter—
some disturbance—comes and the birds
fly wildly. No way to calm them down, no keeper's close attendance,
lights, jungle music, tame twittering of paddock avionics,

only the patternless mad fling of bodies and the engendered memory—
not even memory, only blood spat into the brain—
of vast green tracts and courtly practice, fig trees
filled with purple fruit, birdlings, cuties,
no goshawks in sight, the broad, banded, unbuckled sky
and coherent sunshine luffing calmly, not for them.

Better Than Heaven

So many set-asides, you say, intemperate
millionaires, those responsible for our welfare,
and individuals without malice
who goofed, the jail cells of our misery
damp with the morning chill, you say, done with, ruined,
the worst has happened, those we trusted, trimmers
at Zabar's carving the lox, and the wisdom
of children, finished, comparisons invalid,
the stupefied escape artists
and ministerial candidates and the self-satisfied
disposed of,
the rescued returned to the floods
and fruit pickers, those who catch beauty
aflight on the sweet-smelling breeze, authentic characters
messed up, dead on the floor
of western motels, crapped-out jinxed, lost
to the boulevards, you say, past saving,
charlatans and poseurs, the wise, minxes in damaged fur coats,
drapers and stevedores
watching cartoons reflected in project windows, even
this compared to that, you say, and metaphorically, antique cars
gathering dust in apartment house garages,
old ladies getting sick from their cats, drunks,
homeless women fat on starch, the confused,
young boys ready to die, those still able to capitalize
and producers of change, you say, erased,
gone over, discontinuous, possibly lost,
ruffians and finicky brutalizers
and brilliant talkers, the fake, well-wishers
and party boat captains, those out on bond, the repairmen
just now popping the lids on their coffees, you say,
sailors unmissed drowned, and wives
up for spousal abuse, unaccounted for

now, exhausted in little byways
out of the light, something, you say, better than heaven,
replacement crews undone, lovers hexed, something about this
tremendously appealing, you say, the quiet
in the abandoned mining camps,
the little trails across the desert that turn into artworks,
leads, possible meaning.

Ports of Call

I sink into the arms of a travel brochure
o father
carry me
to far vaguely familiar lands
hydromelic smells
and vistas that don't take too much
from my spiritual
supply
to prevent me
from maintaining the
essential vigil
and afternoon tea with cakes.
I bent the whip
but could not break it.
Storms like pocket geniuses
gather in the corners
and the tectonic welds
fray. We were wrenched from
under gray pines, tossed
into trucks and driven crazy
by minute fractions of our former
happiness revisited.
The fundamental principle
is motion. Yet all this hunger
for a slack still eden.

Check Out Receipt

Schenectady County Public Library - Central
518-388-4500
http://www.scpl.org

Tuesday, Jul 29 2014 10:51AM
30443

Title: Come on rain!
Material: Book
Due: 08/26/2014

Title: When a dad says "I love you"
Material: Book
Due: 08/26/2014

Title: In Secret
Material: New / Popular Book
Due: 08/12/2014

Title: Jump soul : new and selected poems
Material: New / Popular Book
Due: 08/12/2014

Schenectady County Public Library
Central Branch

Who Knows If That Would Work

Repetitions might work, for example
                    the bald Russian vacillator
showing up at the party beat to shit
        wearing a hospital bracelet stamped
                            Unknown Unknown;
or my love's story
where they were never in the milk bar you like so much;
or the double set of figured curtains,
                    rustling as if dawn's conclusive;
or backyard
        and frontyard;
or the river with its matching banks
                        still damp
from rain in which every drop
said the exact same thing—
                    like me
with my fixations and night sweats
rearing from the dust
and acclaim of dreams, my interest in you
        suspect, yet each day
                    revivified, little white boat of love
rounding the bend toot toot.

If Anything Can

Of those dark days

at the end of August, the sky mixed up
befouled grisaille, breeze harvesting rain off to the west—
an imperial, catastrophic weather like bad debts

called in, delicious really,
like works of art where we inhabit pain
and return from it, chastened and lively, as they say,

more than spectacle—so much a part of us—
the gash and run of wind,
the cooled-down damp, the brachiate system

expressing itself like an emotional persistence
amid changes we hardly recognize—
not menacing, only storms

in late summer. Speckled sycamores
tortured by drought. The taxed
and overextended stand bleakly on corners sweating,

wondering what to do, what can be done.

Gain

A backwall of mirrors in a deserted store
show me on my way. Then I'm gone

and they show the street again. It's not
a lonely spot, what with

the falafel vendor and the dessert truck.
In fall leaves blow

from the roof gardens. Rock maple and birch,
catalpa, a few sophora leaves from trees

brought here in jute sacks soaked daily in fresh water
on ships called *Magic Wind*

and *Morven.*
Saplings thin as wands.

In conversation I sometimes claim to be
better than I am. And afterward,

smelling of iodine, in the mirror
yellow in the whites of my eyes, pretend to wonder why.

Monsters

Leaf shadows in the streets, flag shadows winkling
and shuddering, disappearing
then coming back in brightness that seems a new version
of shadow, but it's not, it's only the sun
picking up the pace. Men asleep on the grass,
under trees, it's pleasant now, tranquil
in early morning—pains, spells, hearts eased—wake
to the same batch of trouble but still
a calm like water in a pan left undisturbed all night, dust
on the surface; the little light left burning looks like an ornament now.

Why We're Here

. . . the dramatic reading of my love letters
my secret thoughts in which
I danced with the dictator all night a fretful and uneasy
sort but lovable and now the country classics

are playing my old come-hithers
the sopping costume I wore
for years like a sodality, the pressurized capsule
I spent my summers in

taunting the losers, all these manufactured
houses of love, the crab-walk to the governor's palace,
have come back from the dead—or were never dead they say,
only sapped—the despised and

useless
were really my best friends
and the crapped-out have come to tell me
it's raining in dixie and the gross

taunts I overheard have been converted into well-run niceties
and what was the name of that boy
the fretful child barefoot in the pantry
I popped in the back of the head as I went by.

In the Guest Room

The young man in damson velvet pants
and in the subway the scarred aerialist
I abruptly hugged
and had to hurry away from

lest I be held for questioning—what
are they thinking
right now?
Is he carefully

picking up the new kittens one by one
and examining them
before he drops them in the sack?
Or is she running through

old majorette routines in the mirror
propped on the backporch?
How could those who know us know who we really are?
Even the ones, prescient

and alert, who caught us whispering
curses in the arboretum
or signaling
meekly to a carping lout. They too wish

they could do Father's trick
of whistling through his cupped hands.
They too in their minds
have become trainers of small dogs,

teaching the back flip
and the skipping walk on two legs
that excites
a feeling in them they have described to no one.

Shakespeare in the Villages

It's another dusty afternoon on Godzilla Street.
                The rattled little monarchs and their kin,
the blustery cartoons, what's obvious and about
to take over—something unusual, I guess—
        a stillness betided with grief,
                    someone speaking
with a pal about ducats, ducats and wine,
all this, and the minute fractions
     of temperament,
          the little drawings tossed in the trash,
it's got to mean something,
like an adage,
the give-and-take of the fracas, the way one
     thing without comment replaces another, you saw it,
new people operating the jewelry store,
now it's a shop that sells hampers and buckets, interiors no one's lived in yet.

As Ever As Ever

I step back from the homespun,
the naturally dyed. Fresh vegetables
unnerve me with their husks
and peelings and little ruddy bits
to save for compost. Grass stains
and leaves choke the gutters and
berries ponk ponk and you can't
remember what you were thinking
bark chafes and flesh if you eat it
lies like a lump of chalcedony in
your gut, stopping the action.
Wind grieves at the corners of
the house and rain distills pity
to a purity that is irresistible and
poison. All know a flower's dumb stare.
Fruit is home for small black worms.
Trees thrive in mass groupings
that close behind you and shudder
and stir complex imaginings
we are wholly unsuited for. Better
a quiet nook uptown. A room
with faded yellow light and Monk
on the piano. The buckle
and belting of life are beside the point.

Crossing Washington Square at Dawn

A blank
coverage expressing
movement, heat-

free in Feb,
catches webbed,
sucked-dry branch tips,

opens yellow roads
soon to be sponged up
by hard-

core day. Early
ministrators, lonely convivialists
urging their dogs

to shit. The dauphin
and his bastard
son, pushing

a stroller
piled with documents
proving the succession, smile

as they pass. The old
give-and-take, takes,
gives slightly

like a fat man lifting
off a fart.
Soon everything here

will be sopped up
by time, the bibelots
and usages,

economic systems
rattled to dust. Only art
will last,

the slightly changed
light dogged,
licking the doting words.

Life on Earth

You'd think they planned it, a decrepitude
more unreal by the day, arthritis (fingers locked, shaded to the left),
crippled thoughts in a crippled world, oak shadows smelling of shit,
even flowers, ungerminated, rank, self-poisoned hyacinth turning gray,
museful, crumpled scatterings, mossy cloudbanks of used alyssum
and choked sweet william, piled, torn-up rosebushes—
an area in Central Park where aged florals, worn-out junipers
and other evergreens, are discarded, where the formerly gorgeous
no longer compatible or artful wither.
In fall they're burnt with the trash in capacious bonfires
in sight of Metropolitan Museum windows
letting light in on Pacific war canoes and painted suits of island kings,
arrangements no relation one to the other, except
for those who think constantly of what gets away from us.
Yet even here, even now, some assistant
leaning on his life to come—loss then fade away—makes up his mind.

Blue Pills

. . . wonder about these concoctions delivered to the body,
aching sting
and shrieking sharp crash into the tiny secret rooms
where deserters lie sobbing, where,

sweaty and profound, the burdensome toils
occur,
the stacks of matériel and the corpuscular
dominations plug on and play out, aided—

saved—by these
wormwoods and unripe olive
assaults. I smell of loneliness
and manual labor. The hardy convincers, the dead

ends and exsiccated shooting galleries
where we smoked crack
and lay on gutshot mattresses caressing each
other's skinniness

are gone.
The officious proletariat of the soul
and the mud-spoilt faces are dead.
Nowhere in this world

to run to. Cold blue
Mexican heavens
where Villa plunges his hands up to the elbow
in a longhorn's chest. A minute ago

the heart was beating.
A minute ago the eyes held up
buckets of light. Almost nothing, Villa says,
between here and nothing.

The Plot Is the One Thing We Know

Some record put together
of individual
          portions

the slick monkey paw leaves

          and arrested
          growth in the backlogged

pines somebody says *would you look at*

that
and you wonder what
                    pass by without

          finding out the little

appurtenances soft sensibilities
you employ

                    to escape the brechtian
                    possibilities
                              the empty city pools

they used for arenas

and now

          they're comfortably
                              returned from

prison
the huge pads

over the eyes the blank spaces
between here

and the hinges—

outside the world's

battered
and ready
for the fryer—

> *you take*
> *a little hit*

my father says
            from his grave
                        and you go on

under the folds of the earth the caesars
sid and julius
constitutionalists

the overly prepared

churning in the afterwash

of whatever
it was
propelled all this.

Collected First Lines

I'm not saying I'm confused by the way a flock
of blackbirds makes me think
an organization's moving its headquarters,

but I wonder about the elusive silvery momentum
of certain fish, animals
avoiding sunlight, the way a river cracks

open into white, discursive signatures;

I'm not opposed to valuable heirlooms
found tucked in a sack of potatoes,
the cleric's garb and two-tone shoes
in the whore's back room;

I'm not surprised at wasted days,
whole seasons spent in the wrong house;

I've positioned myself near the suicide's regalia,
the sharpened blade, the pistol, the noose
(I like to poke these items with the toe of my boot);

I've taken the measure of certain lost causes,
resisted in a quiet way the release

of records that would shed an unhappy light on the case;

I've half deliberately lost my way,
exchanged pitiful glances, curried favor
with undeveloped bloodlines, dogged it;

I've compared notes with fools and found myself wanting;

I'm not claiming a special privilege,
I don't want my back pay;

I caught myself staring into a barrel
and was unable to confirm what I saw there;

as in the misplaced manifesto,
I'm sure there is meaning,
and I know it's sometimes more interesting
to stand in a road than to move along it,

though even this, said with such confidence
just a minute ago,

explains nothing.

Just a Note

fall picks at the sycamores

and the rain attempts to insert its ringless fingers into the padlocked
summer suitcases that when prized open

reveal in their vast bogs where the setbacks are stored,
the slackjawed corpses
that never learned the lingo, whole civilizations packed in the dead mouths

of those who mixed up what they valued
with a tinkling sound they heard as a child, who at odd times

remembered flowering dogwoods floating among the pines
and a reticence they were unable to shake, even at the trials that stood in

for their lives, who found

the swimming pools shuttered
under brown canvas, burger stands closed, and the lifeguards fled to Florida.

On Down

Streets with their heads in one river, feet in the other,
      private as thoughts at this time of day, apportioned,

the reserves almost used up—thoughts, that is—old-timers
        expiring, letting the vast encumbrages go, the willies, investitures

and soldierly nights walking the baby, something always coming like an appointment
      in Massapequa, the little fruits on the apple trees

squinched and striped, still sweet—if you take the time to pick them—
        the usefulness of things debatable, the oncoming trains,

the particularities and ships in the harbor
      relieved of great cargoes, reefers filled with cedar chips and tars,

age coming, weather not much different from what was here last year,
      or is it the troublesome storm we evaded in Freeport, the little periodicities

like a rationing of shore lights, the boats gone awry, old approaches worn,
      the centralities mussed like a lover's hair.

2. HOUSE TRAILER IN A FIELD

Little Georgias

All these books I don't read anymore like the towns
I no longer go to, racked burgs
and hamletitos, gateways to loneliness—Bible readers
flipping pages to find the passage that reads
HEAVEN OPEN: FREE TO ALL, tiny grim children
sucking the heads of miniature dolls
as if stunned in sandy side streets
their parents like trees with the bark
stripped by lightning up one side, abjectly dying,
and those rainy afternoons in winter that stick in the mind
like something out of Dante
or Thorstein Veblen, the whole house damp,
the rain drilling into its one
hundred and fifth day, only Arnell Williams,
wrapped in a torn pineapple quilt,
trudging through the sand drifts on her way to the package store.

Used to Be More One-Eyed Men

. . . . used to be more one-eyed men,
more crippled men and obscure backward men
half-crazy from teasing,
who did their personal business in an alley
and came up later with powdered sugar on their lips
asking questions
about lightning, used to be women
who scrubbed clothes with corncobs,
who stood amply foursquare, used to be men
without purpose continuing on, used to be women
turned into wraiths, and naked boys throwing rocks,
used to be a long way to the river, we'd ride the mules,
used to be a timeless sense to life,
used to be horrible occurrences just over the ridge,
women mutilating dead enemies, men
pissing in another man's eyes, used to be the grime
wouldn't come off, the waste was interminable,
used to be the jealous uncle
still alive, plotting revenge, used to be
less pavement, villages without sidewalks,
used to be a path through the fields to the lover's house,
used to be drunks and solitaries sleeping on the docks,
used to be elevated talk, phrasings like
varnished yachts turning in the canal, flowers in bunches
left on the porch, there were intricate performances,
felicities without justification or reason, used to be
a farmer fell in love with a town girl and never spoke of it,
not for forty years, and later, after he died,
you could ponder the corpse laid out on the bed,
and there was always some cousin rifling the boxes,
used to be a diary you came on with stilted confessions,
the love of a woman barely discernible in the bad writing
and choked-off feelings, used to be someone

would scarcely realize what this farmer had gone through,
someone almost not related who rocking on the porch later
recalled a phrase from the diaries,
something about what the farmer *saw*,
and understood he loved a woman,
used to be this was enough, a memory like this
passed down haphazardly from father to son, later
worked out in a story or a script, a grain of it alive
in the heart of one ambitious for fame
or simply peace, used to be you
could repeat this in your own life obscurely,
experience the tender insistence, the weird, crippled hope.

It Gets a Little Hazy

The years in Cuba are behind me now.
Little spotted dogs, like tiny archangels
followed me around. I smelled of salt
and palm oil. Given the nature

of belief, the effectiveness of the divine will,
unforgettable and strictly
for the birds, I could be said
to be out of touch. I read Aeschylus—

the diaries—*Othello on the Beach*,
and Peter Gunn. I gave my change
to private charities, something personal
I devised. Her lipstick

smelled like a clown's face. We practiced
tricks the Ringling Brothers taught her.
I supported small retainers,
converts and muralists struggling with

the dialect. We waked,
often at dawn, and lay
in the sheets cursing quietly. *I will
particularize and dissuade*, she said,

but it made no difference. I wore hats
of coconut frond and drove a Russian car.
My retreat from life
fit like a glove. Some nights

strange memories, passing for dreams,
of mud-caked shoes, cats

on the table eating scraps, and young men
caressing the faces of their superannuated lovers.

I shivered sometimes. I was on a long run
of quirky asides. *Take the monkey,* she said, *and go.*

Green Life Where It Goes

I go off and visit the trees,
the gray-green one,
and the complicated cucumber tree
I thought was a magnolia.
Late fall's an explanation
someone's left off arguing about,
a declamation on a lonely corner
around suppertime, unprovable.

You can go on telling someone
their ragged and misinformed
way of looking at things
won't wash, but they never
listen. You have to
step out into the yard,
really get into the stars, the dew
and the peacock cries.
It will probably get better,
though there's no guarantee of this,
and besides, today's the day.

Where's my frothy ebullience
now when I really need it? What
helps if not dreaming about real estate,
about sunlight on blue formica tables,
and bare tanned legs? Someone,
somewhere, is entering his heyday.
He'll go on through it
to the sick coughing and regrets
of eventide, but why furnish
your head with that just yet?
There's no way to be careful enough.

From the middle distance a shout—
warning or hopeful cry?—
perhaps a friend wants to let us know
he's about to start up
again. I didn't know I could
grieve love's loss
so long, I had no idea.
Find someone else, a friend says,
but I can't, or won't;
I'd like to cry every tear first.
Or simply not let go.
Or pretend absence is presence,
that old routine. The day leans
against me and asks for a light.
I'll follow green life where it goes.
I enjoy saying this and rub the heel
of my hand with my good thumb,
think about an aria I heard
where the tenor went on past
the grief into a credible exactitude
vis-à-vis solace and hope. A silence
fell then, not stunned exactly, but as if
those around him didn't know what to say.

Night Squishes the Sun Out Along the Treeline

I left out of there in a Pontiac I stole from one of my brothers and drove until I was too tired to go on. In a field in Virginia I rested under some oaks and watched a rolling flock of blackbirds devise another entrance point into the mystery of being. After a while I drove on to a little town where the mayor was hanging his laundry on a line beside the house. He said he knew me but this was not true. I gave him a sandwich and we sat on his front steps talking about the ruins of our lives. He harped on alignment and succulence, I spoke my piece about the universal buttering up going around. We sat there until the stars had wheeled around to face the other way. You could smell the asphalt plant across town. Time's rusty chains held us as we leaned back into our solitudes like children on a barge hauling them downriver to their worthless foster homes.

Before We Get There

Those with an unsettling mastery are my heroes and dukes in dusty boots
and Victor Hugo-style clerics
who break into tears
of covalence when you talk about somebody's sister
dying of cancer. I get alarmed
when things seem to be piling up like the brow of a hill
about to fall on me. I have to stop
picturing the Mexican high desert
as some kind of heaven. Horses, dry stream beds floored with yellow rock,
dove shoots, and smoky mesquite fires.
I want to let these
paradisos go. I want to sit in the front seat
of my buddy's old Buick
after everyone else has gone inside.
It's summer again
and we're feckless and loose in our thinking and
I'm outrageously happy—or I think I am—
and the windshield has specks in it like tiny crystal stars
shining in daylight
and I know all about what's coming.

Turpentine

Of pine tar, clear glue, a sap
running freely yet quickly curdled white in the bucket

and boiled down in kettles out in the woods
to a thinned juice, upgrader

and extender of intensities, solvent, sustainer
of paints and medicines, of naturalized

and useful fluids generally. Old folks
used it on cuts, scrapes,

to repair the body broken by falls
and gunshots, Uncle Somebody rising

from the swamp torn by a bear. You'd hear him
hollering, nothing particularly unusual

about it, a general claim, exaction of the universe
by a fellow traveler: *Help me, Lord,*

or *Quit, now,* or just *Ay-ee!*
as one might say, raising the shade on Judgment Day.

The River

I was supposed to fly down to see my brother,
but I got sidetracked by some girls
and was two days late. The place was shut up
and my brother was gone to the river to be
with the mangroves & the knobby-headed egrets.
Down there the sun is so bright you can tell
that time will have no trouble with any of us.
I looked for a key to the house, but couldn't
find it and went to see a broker who tried to
sell me the patch of woods we played in as boys.
I didn't want the woods that were monstrous
and filled with demons and the vapors of rot.
He wanted me to drink with him but I wouldn't.
I have to find my brother, I said, and he laughed
and said, *You have no brother*, and I didn't
know what he meant, but I do now. I have
started for the river so many times, but some-
thing always comes up and I turn aside like
one who hears a band playing. Love is the key
to my brother's house, but he is gone to the river.

Whom Mothers Steer Their Children From

At eight what to wear was my big concern,
whether the jeans
with yellow cavalry stripe

crayoned into the seam, or my engineer
boots with ankle strap
and stainless steel rusting buckle,

or whether
to wear a hat
as the men did, soft snap-brims

that concealed
their faces from anyone spying above,
or a cap

with white letter J on it
for the local baseball Jays,
a set of farm team

weepers who never won a game.
Since I was four I'd
been a worrywart, nervous about

failure and edgy,
scared I would turn crazy and throw the cat
in the river

like Joe David Sims,
or slip matches into my pocket
to burn down

the Katy woods,
a tense boy
with motives he couldn't understand,

who in the gleaming dusk
watches across the paved road
as firemen

uncoil their grim hoses,
smiling calmly
to himself—hatted, in boots

and cavalry pants—as flames streak
up pine tree flanks
to catch the birds in their nests.

October Memorial

Fizzles and peculiar latches
let go in the graybeard trees.
Squirrels hang upside down
as life packs it in,

plunges headfirst into the dark's blue flame.
The sides and tops of hills
patted until they go quiet
and fruit trees wrapped in white gowns

like brides.
Customers stand in the grocery store window
looking out as if they are on a train
passing. Smell of mangoes

and pineapple in the bins.
What's left of my brother
a slightly greasy powder
and bone giblets the smell of an old campfire.

In paradise, cola de cameron
and frangipani flowers
float on the surface of the swimming pools
and a few extremely well-realized splashes

hang for hours
like shining white epergnes, custom made.

This Before That

The hacked-off, split, misfired sycamores
crazed by drought, offering crimped, dusty
versions of spumed futurities, the tiny wires
and orifices shriveled at the base—trounced
by spring dancing on a tractor wheel. Abelias,
like over-handled brides, sample the air,
trembling, in their roots preparing the channel
by which life will flee to freedom. Headlong
into the dark is what's offered, tools and directions extra.

Toward the end the days bunch up,
picturesque afternoons in water meadows
and bus tours to Essex where Constable hid his materials,
no longer available. Everyone knows this.
The faint desecrations and put-ons, short orders
rescinded, the close examination of elemental particles,
the approach, shimmy and begin to fade. Obscure noises,
as if from the dispatch unit of an army lost years ago
in backyard exercises, begin to filter through.
What are they saying? you wonder,
and remember that was what you wondered then.

Spell

I see about half the spell life's put on me, maybe less.
A bird singing fully wild tunes in the pittosporum,
a creature so close, a regular, issuing its indecipherable bulletins,
reliable, compact, interposed between me
and the roar in my head; it's something to be grateful for.

I wake up thinking I'm nearly done and fear bites me like a dog.
Sun's already slipped in among the ruellia and the ficus,
I taste dust from old, rarely visited cities in my mouth.
Philosophies, kingdoms, swim through my eyes
like prison fields glimpsed from a passing pickup truck.

Thoughts Like a Series of Night Departures

There's a delicate, disorderly understanding coming to light
behind the cattle barns, and offers have been made on the boulevards
that confirm the age's irrepressible spirit. Desire quickens,
brushes by us, and fades. After the rain we walk to the park.
Breeze shakes water from the palms and begins
in the highest branches of pines its speculations on the nature of light.
A softened and poorly delineated sadness,
a passivity in certain quiet fumblings, in the drooped heads of mallows,
the way the band of saffron light shades into a lower and depleted purple brushing,
the delight we take in the sound of each other's voice, the way
our love for a moment reiterates a larger grace,
the sea smell, two small children beating a large blue barrel with sticks,
beating their enemies, beating joy loose, beating time into rhythm,
the matted damp grass from which tiny green flies lift
and wobbling take flight, all that is left over
from the day's series of wrecks and repairs, from speculation
and the passed-over bruised fruits of misunderstandings and fretful
disorganized pleadings, from life sunk to the ears,
misapplied and delighted in, all is touched by the same
confounded, apparent and diminishing tenderness.

Red Cotton

My wife's in the kitchen melting plastic spoons,
I'm out back
coaxing the cat out of a mincemeat pie.
Symbolically in these matters we're connected—
like captains on distant windjammers,
one on fire,
the other signaling for a second helping.

I smell of pecans—a slightly sour
odor like rusted license plates.

Lately, I like to drive around town in the notary's car,
the world's smallest. He kept a snake
under the backseat, but the snake died.
The remains have a dusty old garbage smell,
and faintly, when I turn the corner, rattle.

I still don't know what kind of man I am.

I press my lips to red cotton,
red cotton panties, and sigh.

Fresh Rolls on Sunday

I slip out among the buds
and incomplete blossoming,
do my turnarounds and twirls,
my fake dance steps to catch
the upthrusts and partial
infiltrations of passionflower
and potato vine. Everywhere
the light's taking apart the dark,
not stopping to rake up
the pieces. The eternal
shines like silver dimes
in the grass. The soul's free
radicals, slippery like birch sap,
coat the backs of passing speckled
butterflies. Everyone
knows that the world,
still indifferent to special treatment,
grants itself compensation for
the trouble it's gone to. Collapsed
hillsides smell like fresh bread.
And daffodils, heavy as anvils,
anchor the feet of the dead.

3. EAST WASHERWOMAN SHOAL

Delirious

In Miami
not a moment too soon
the hookers
who don't want to be alone yet
ask if I'd like a little morning massage
the sun's rising
like someone stepping from a barroom fight
the pace is killing
and just right like the sound of songbirds
as the clouds dissolve
everything's trying to keep a lid
on the terror
be good about the gaps
those bright bits broken off the fuselage
maybe they're new stars
like gods
from the other side of the world
throwing bodies in the air
catching fire
there's a list
we're always adding to
ours
and the one we're on

Originality (1)

Between two stained condo pods they've left
a preservation tract you can slump through on
a sullied board path hammered loosely
into the tangle, take a gander at the undefended
scrub, the area's originality a shabby plot
containing strangled greasy waterway stained orange
by rootwork fingerling snappers and other
life-charged get probe and dash through taking
on weight. Halfpint trees, grimy and tired of life
like cozened migrants shoved into backdoor cuddies
cramped tiny verminous with old spallings
slaked from the ceiling and blocked plumbing,
grown-up gray in the face, going bald.
Biotic debris and moiled sopping human trash,
dead rats and insect husks the tide's too feeble
to suck out to sea litter sandy patches that smell.
Abruptly you reach the canal separating polder
from development. On the other side glass-fronted
houses squint at the sun. Punch-drunk children
slathered with bug repellent push their strollers
off the dock and watch them sink into the slough.

Originality (2)

From the rank salt swamp you break eventually
into full sunshine that even to one practiced
in tropical matters seems overdone. Drenched
pricked cut sloshed under convulsing mosquito
swarms you follow the busted boardwalk that bends
like an illusion of mockery and raving through
a gnawed (or clawed) buttonwood scrub. Bleak
sandy patches strewn with quern vomitings lie
like pounded facial plates left untreated,
edged with ebb trash, exploded trumpery,
rotten sargassum weed and stabbed bleach bottles.
A fishing boat's crushed transom awaits
the coming of a better age. Stink-clung bones,
batting, puffed gray clotted shit and mucosal
muck hang in the bushes. The stretch ends in
a scummed-over slough that smells and you can't
cross. Nothing to do but turn around. When you
get back and they ask, you say you had to be alone.

Taps in Key West

Up-tipped, half-stoved-in barrel crusted with white cochinas,
that's the island, calcific, glozed to a sheen, bobbing in the Gulf's backstream.

Proleptic, grazed by dawn, a lank breeze rouses in the mangroves
and stirs the herons into life. Day unrolls like a towel with all the states

painted on it, or a love letter composed in barbecue sauce, marked up
with stipulations and bughouse claims, handwriting like a kidnapper's,

IN CAPITALS, each word with a stupefied silence before and after.
This winter gamefish washed by thousands to the sidelines and the manatees

sank like adiposal gangsters shod in cement. Now spring's hacked itself
loose and the trees shoulder their gaudy epaulets. Birds like painted thumbs

nicker at the rooflines. The sun builds its coliseum. In the cemetery
dew daisies and yellow hawksbeard bristle, ready to repel armies of the dead.

Supposition

Lately I've throttled back, like a burglar
changing his face, one dab,
one touch of eye gloss, at a time.

I drive by the graveyard to visit Mother,

but she's still not there. I make sorties
to the mall, investigate a high-pitched whine,

buy milky-blue curtains and stop at the ocean
to see if they match. Sudsy swells
and oblates, the casual way a heron snaps up a fish,

the stink of sea grass, press against my knowledge of what's coming
like the din from a shift in government
in a country where we failed to beat the charges.

I sense the phantom musculature surrounding
old love affairs,
now warped and peeling like wooden tennis rackets. I entreat

the dusk with its genial
dispersals, its sun faded to a reference in the pittosporum.

Comely, not at all foreign,
dereliction presents the bill.

My soul, faded to jells and darns,

drapes like a thrift store shawl
across the shoulders of my ex-wife's old Pontiac.

Rummage

Little lanes besotted with themselves—Lost Haircut, Poorhouse—
each bush, celeriac tree, whiskered creature softly pawing
a spoiled guava a witness to its own establishing shot,
the soul's linkage each moment underived, essential services
underplayed but still apt, the rain that comes each afternoon
bringing from the transfer stations of the sea something new
we're on the lookout for. Little lanes, perfidious and selective,
trumped by an aside, cumbrous, leaden-footed promises, you say,
this love like a treehouse on a leafy cul, up among the swirls
and desecrations of thought, a whim become a way of life,
and now, among the tides and placement services of the spirit-
guides, the rake-offs out of which we pay the help, themselves
forcing hopefulness into faith, rummaging for a loophole.
Soon the fragrant airs of early morning will pass, replaced
by little stinks and tinctures of alteration, the dwindling
carriage tapering to what's irreplaceable, the frets and fumes.

Don Diego de la Vega on Block Patrol

Out here the day's already in place,
the spiky efflorescence, the particularly gifted
established with an air of frivolous permanence
without substance, the botanical curios
and steady providers,
the cattle of the plant world, and small, portly
dogs waddling,
poking their faces into happiness,
providing inconclusive
evidence of possibility among the growing shade
and false sturdiness of the complex conjugate,
the undergirding already accepting donations
of excess baggage and spoiled fruit,
the pathways still greasy
with tromped-on excrescences,
the tainted articles of dubious manufacture
rusting separately, and the confused
widowers long awake,
rattled children attempting showdowns
that will end badly, crows picking up
the pace, a bewildering scatter of poisonous berries,
degraded, overpainted bracts and panicles,
the old primary school, long deserted,
increasing the sense of the shameful and fated
encrustations of ignominy
in this era of lies, of life meretriciously lived
by those disposed to it and needled by dread.

What's Essential

these little scratches I got
or the light shattered on the islands

duplicity or ransom notes
smeared by rain so you can't read the amount

and leave only 47.50 in a suitcase under the old bridge.
It's gonna be okay. We've still

got time. That little flashfire
you burned the papers in

didn't catch the roof. *What agony,* she said,
and ate another slice of pie. I got this wind

at my back, relatively
speaking, and the lagoon's not that deep anyway.

Squirrels in the coconut palms.
How's it possible we can get far enough away

so we think we've gotten away? At least for a while?
These stacks of

emollients,
anesthetics, shape-shifters

and the like. I got to go.
We were reading Shakespeare

when the bear came into the yard.
Martha saw him out the window.

He only
wanted to look around. Bottom-heavy,

waddling, wearing a fur coat in summer,
you had to wish him well.

Water in the Lungs

Durable like the souls
of fishermen in the backcountry, old-timers

in weathered gear, complainers and the hardy
ex-basketball players and short guys

griping about the heat, the turnaround in such a life
explicit in gravure and stain, the accomplice wave action

and soft scudding of breeze on some days
when the sun lays a hard gloss on the water and you recall,

as if they've never stopped, the faint cries of the drowned,
who bear down on their memories as on the bodies

of former lovers off somewhere in a scalding heaven of their own,
everything they ever knew a mystery received

and applied to what's following, to butterfish and scup,
to the salt slick and final

on a wrist once absentmindedly
caressed by a young mother as she licked a fresh hook into gleaming.

Bus to Tuxtla

Sometimes you wait a while for the bus—
the bus of happiness
probably—just now passing the fried pie hutch
or crossing the stream like an old lady
carefully lifting her knees from the water—bus of transversal
and hopefulness—sometimes you wait all afternoon
and into the twilit hours, when, as time reverses slightly,
you feel the scarlet undergarments brush your cheek
as they go by, as the vastness disguised as a young girl passes,
sometimes, as the bus that is entering the outskirts of the ancient city
you've loved but never been at home in, bus with the face
of a tiger painted on the front, growling
to a stop at the marshy local park
where an old woman slowly growing used to being alone
waits quietly—sometimes, like a man of weary but unconquerable faith,
you wait all your life for the bus with its equipage of silver
rods and checked-cloth seats, its companionable
or fractious passengers, some growing weary now,
some broken beyond repair, others still hoping for an easement—
wizard or laundress—one for whom the door,
with an exculpatory gush, will open,
and as one ascending the last few steps into heaven
will rise, dreaming of a breeze lifting
slender curls of new vine in the old vineyard
that's gone now, and grasp the silver rod like the impossible means
into a paradise once hoped for on earth and nearly
found one afternoon among sequins and discarded undergarments
under a tamarind tree with a lover
who's dead and faded to haze and misremembered gestures—
and find a seat,
and just now, not long before the bus
reaches her stop,
disappears like the Mixotec kings into time.

Dengue

Mosquito implanted little fleurs-de-lis
probably in my right wrist unnoticed really
when the unwiped pump dumped energetic
wrigglers in the vein. A few days later
I put my head down on the table
and slept three hours. Fever a seething
hydrous wind that blew the house doors wide.
I sank in a scalding vessel suddenly caught
in the ice capades, the crew collapsed and
baldly illuminated, all souls skinned
and left rotting on a sunbaked portico.
I couldn't talk or go outside or eat.
You could cook an egg on my forehead, with
a side of fries. Gainful, prim, my soul
slipped out the back hauling the collectibles.
Only the stink of tainted meat and bananas left.
Swept in a clumsy current, basted, super-
factuated, raked by voices commemorating
the loquacity of drowned privateers and painters
whose work had been burned by the judges,
I lay on the bed panting. They set me trussed
in a hole and dumped liquid nitro into me,
fed me cheese. The graveclothes no longer fit
and I was sorry. Cunning fingers probed
deeply into areas I'd claimed were blank.
The fever rolled like a horse in the dust.
It took a year before I could sing Dixie.

As If You Were

flat broke, you might say.
anyway I can see the ocean from here. lifted

monstrance, shipped and salivating,
it shows its tiny ridged teeth, the calm of interludes

like the secret place inside the heart's
curvature. the way an instant wants to loop back

and profess, the way
I am almost able to say

what the ringing bells might
want of me, the charm, the pleasure

in a raked-back autumn sky,
the way the circumstance, the piled logs

and pleasure craft misused
and stranded, the carefully detailed

obscurities coming forward
like ex-gangsters now selling flowers by the old beach road,

the flat-handed breeze
adding its sketchy

trembling, the basic news still pretty much the same,
somebody carrying a hamper of old standards,

the boys walking around on the sand singing
parts of the remaining hymns, the ocean memorizing everything,

slapping its hands
and boasting without moving its lips,

the frankness that comes
over you

when the noise dies down. I mean
the honesty. the way your eyes light up,

the ruckle, the tuck, the flexure,
everything suddenly precious.

Offhand

The heat creeps in like a ghost ship,
releasing its vaporous crew to overrun the town.
Something like this on Friday last. Shadows digging
a tunnel to freedom, the sun's constant shelling wearing
us down. I gather my old burgundy robe about me,
totter to the kitchen for a drink of ad hominem.
Bullace flowers drift through the garden
like souls on their way to the convenience store.
I'm older than I ever was, younger than
I'll ever be again. My luggage waits
on the porch, the sample cases I'm returning.
I didn't get that far into things, the murks
and rackets, but I liked the grassy
salients I sometimes stood on gazing at the water.

SELECTED POEMS

from RED ROADS

Dr. Auchincloss Bids Good-bye to His Wife

There is a jukebox in New Orleans
that plays Beethoven's *Eroica* and it
is toward that jukebox or symphony I am
walking, down a white sidewalk upon which the rain
has begun to cancel
the catalpa leaves, larger than hearts, lime green,
like the ambitious stamps of some Caribbean countries, and,
as I hoped it would, the air smells of decay,
of the river's two-thousand-mile journey
dragging its own corpse, which it will heave
this evening
into the obliterating brown waters
of the Gulf of Mexico. On the corner is a restaurant
where for three dollars they will bring you a plate
heaped high with the obsidian bodies
of crawfish. The crawfish, steamed in bay leaves,
will keep you from starving, though, someone
is always protesting, nothing, *nothing*
really keeps you from starving. There is some
principle of light
flicking across the wedding ring of the banjo player
on the corner, and I would love
to understand this
principle, as I would love to understand
the blond woman shaking out a quilt
on the red balcony at the end of the street.
I can walk all the way down St. Charles
without speaking to anyone, and it is possible
to be grateful, for the delicacy of passersby,

who do not seem to mind. That symphony
begins with three great notes
like the gates of the ocean
breaking down, but when it is over,
and we are pressing our fingers through the water rings
on the glass-topped table
and craning for the waiter, who has gone to the john,
it will still be Sunday
and the blue evening
will be testing its grip once more
at the heart of our lives.

Liar

What brings me alive
is less than simplicity,
is a company of soldiers in shiny blue jackets
boiling chickens in the shade
by the Erasmus Gate, is the fact that my grandfather
died begging for mercy
in a hotel in Atlanta, and that my grandmother, in 1910,
mourned because her breasts
were small.

I know four men
who paddled the length of the Mississippi
in a dugout they hacked
and burned out of a beech tree. When anyone mentioned rivers
they would look at each other
and their eyes would soften with the memory
of mists and sandbars,
of the grave black brows of river barges.

I come from a country as large as Brazil,
but all I remember
are the wet silver webs
of golden jungle spiders
netted in the cane.

I wake up thinking of my brother,
who, on a July morning in 1954,
killed a boy without meaning to.
And I can tell you that this isn't true,
that my brother didn't,
as he swept back a four iron
on the lawn of our house in Sea Island,
crack the temple of a boy we had only met

the night before. I can say Yes
I am lying again,
about the boy, about Sea Island,
but as you get up to fix another drink
I will tell you a story
about sleeping in a hay barn in Turkey
and of waking in the night, as, one by one,
the farmhands stood out of the rank straw
to greet us.
                    I want you to know
that my life is a ritual lie
and that I deserve to be loved
anyway. I want you to smile
when I tell of the purple hyacinths
caught in the gears of the raised bridge
over the Chickopee River, I want you to pretend
you were there.

My sister's hips were two ax handles wide,
she wept that no one would love her,
my sister, who waded among yellow poppies
and wondered if she were really alive—I want you to wish
you had married her,
I want you to say Please, why did she leave me,
Get her back, O my God,
how can I live without her. I'm not even amazed
that I want you to say this. Listen,
I came downstairs this morning
and somebody had filled the house with flowers.

from INDISTINGUISHABLE FROM THE DARKNESS

Aquarium

After the sporty dolphin show
you might wander down the dimmed aqua stairs
into a darkness they have cut windows
through, to see beyond the foggy glass
all fishes swimming. It's not a glass bowl,
but like the earth itself cut through,
so that you are a traveler
rising from the interior to this first glimpse
at the teeming world. They circle slowly: sharks,
yellow jack, angelfish; a stately manta pumps
its black wings, soars toward
the chopped surface, sinks into a turn, and disappears.
It is some kind of lion-with-the-lamb business,
all these varieties, cold killers and dumb
swimmers, schoolers, the lonely blue-throated
pilot fish, speckled distraught octopi
jammed under rocks. You have come out of sunlight
maybe, from the jaunty tricks
of trained porpoises who ring bells and
toss a ball and bark like crazy dogs, but down here
where it smells like the seabed, and your schooling neighbors
move shadily to grasp—as that man does—the
sills of small rectangular portals, holding
tightly as if onto the railing
above a gorge, and the slab side of a grouper
slides into view and you see the black incurious eye unblinking,
and the next,
and the light shafts down
to strike the hard back of a channel bass,

the cocked fin of a sawfish, you discover
another version of privacy in this voyeur's
den; like walking in on your father after the operation,
where as the black monitor ticks
its sad declarations you meet the gray dragged face,
the gray hand groping at the broken dorsal of his sex,
the gray, foolish smile he lifts and lets go
in the dust-stirred, murky room
that is like a tank you are both trapped in.

Fortune

At a small monastery—or what had been
a monastery—outside Obregón, we stopped;
you were suffering the hollow nausea of your first
pregnancy, sleeping as best you could
through the thousand miles of pines
and rocky fields of northern Mexico, so I went ahead
through the saddle-colored rooms, past
the broken church and the row of empty sheds,
where Indian women, according to a sign,
once baked the flatbread called *sapatos de María*,
to a garden in the back, over the parapet of which
I could see the river through some willows: a rinsed
bed of sand, dry now in winter.
                              I didn't want a child,
and I was tired of closeness, tired
of being kind, so was glad to be alone
a while and lay down under a jacaranda tree,
and watched through leaves the changing pattern
of the sky, which I was tired of too, the scaly, stratospheric
winter clouds, edged with light, like the tiny waves
you pointed out, reflected on the bottom of a bridge
we rowed under in a rented boat, the day you told me
of the child—I was tired and slept.

It was nearly evening when I woke, two mestizo women
hurried talking through the tulip beds, the sky was pale.
They'd set small plaques among the plants,
naming them, the ornamentals and the fruit. Some,
so the writing said, were descendants
of the cuttings brought from Spain by monks;
intermingled here—Pinot grape with ocotillo,
damascene rose—they thrived. I thought of a certain
tenderness, and forbearance, a man might bring

to vines and simple vegetables, cultivated
in memory of his home perhaps, in a foreign place;
and thought how sometimes what passes on from us
has little to do with what we hoped, but nonetheless
carries word of who we were and what we found.
For a moment then, among the arbors and the flower beds,
I did not feel so distant from this time and place,
and the edge of my own local fears began to dull.
I plucked a sprig—a leaf was all—
from a holly bush, and brought it out to you,
a little stronger in a portion of myself, a little
reconciled, though I couldn't know then
that in a month we would lose the child,
and in time you would pass,
like a squandered fortune, from my life.

Transformation to White

Some stranger's
clever, coincidental conversation
is preparing me
for solitude; it rises and fades
as I step onto the avenue where just down there
trees shaped like the entrances to caves
are barring the light from this side of Manhattan.
Sometimes I want to pass completely

unnoticed through my life, I want to become
like the melted light
pouring down on the roofs of cars, filling
the street and the windows,
then fading. In a minute

I will pause under the fruit-choked trees
bandaging a derelict house on Eleventh
to speak a small sermon
on the redundancies of joy.
I believe, though crushed and
randomly derelict, we might yet
thrust our hands into abundance
& be provisioned. Darkness has slipped out

among us, and the first lightning bugs of summer,
blinking over the miniature gardens of Manhattan, tremble
and sway. I could tell you I am tired
of marriage, of ambition,
and effort, but who isn't, and how
would that explain my survival
and make its triumph touch you? Nearby new apartments
go up in something called the Memphis style;
they are salmon-colored with curved, snapped-on

balconies, harmoniously
advertised, but no one happy with his life
would live there, no one would want
to pass from this world
through the Sheetrock surfaces and pale
hallways of the Memphis
style. Tonight I will pay seven

dollars to see a woman sit before me
naked, and I am glad I live in a world where a woman
will do this, so simply, making
small talk as she strokes her shaved cunt.
Her breasts are fragile, as soft
as the skin of a baby: the relic,
unveiled flesh through which we might touch
the perfection
we once were. But this thought too
I cast aside, uneasy
with its effortless and dated
resolution. It isn't childhood I'm
looking for from the women
clustered near the piers—it's something older, and worse. Nonetheless,

sated with the spill of jism, I will be
satisfied, momentarily relieved
again; I will thank her
honestly, and a smile will slide out between us,
not the smile of those who hope for twinship,
or for the union of congruent souls,
but of those for whom the paying of debts,
the unpretentious carrying through
of a simple exchange,
has become enough. As I come
she will be speaking of a beach in Florida
she visited with her husband. She will say

it was sunset when they knelt by the water
and touched each other's face
with salt. "I could see the moon
shining on us," she will say. "It was the color of pearls,
and it turned us, and everything near us, white."
Maybe I will hear her voice

later as I grope toward sleep. Maybe, as the body
of my wife turns once more,
so that I feel brushing my back
the shape of the flesh I know best in the world,
maybe I will hear, as I did for a moment then,
the simplified eloquence
of a humanness
so apparent, so undistilled,
that I cannot resist it.

Kohaku

The first time we made love
we crawled away from your brother's campfire
on Carabelle Beach and lay down under a thin blanket
among the burnt pine stumps. You were fourteen
and I was sixteen, younger
than any lovers we ever knew
in the world. For years I thought I had ruined you.
Even after we married
and later divorced and both of us had gone on
to two more marriages apiece, I thought
I had taken something from you that night
and all the other nights, when we lay down in cornfields,
in the bitter yellow grasses by the road,
in your aunt's sun-dusty attic bedroom—and your body,
so pale it seemed sometimes almost transparent,
turned to me, came harshly
against me as if ridden by a will of its own—even then
I thought I had stripped you of choice
in some way, taken only out of selfishness
and desire. I suppose that's my own
lookout now and is only a dry question
from the past that can go without answering.
We broke up, went into the world, grew desperate,
found each other again and, in a rush
of affection and relief, married. We moved
to the mountains, to a white house set into a notch
above a shallow stream. I fished for trout, picked
apples with the local orchard-men; you taught
school. In the evening we walked across the steep pasture
I helped the landlord clear of rocks on Saturdays.
I remembered turning over a stone
the size and shape of a loaf of bread to find a black
widow spider underneath. Its ruby helix

shone like a jewel
from some lost kingdom. It was so beautiful
I wanted to give it to you,
but I crushed it under my boot instead.
In the winter,
as ice inched out into the stream, you grew nervous
and I grew sullen. We took sudden,
hair-raising trips to Philadelphia
and the Yucatán. In spring
we planted a garden, lost
it to beetles. You made flowers
out of red paper that you set like lanterns
in the cedar trees. From the porch at night
I would watch them, their color faded white
and ghostly, shivering and bobbing
in the breeze, and think of Japan,
of intimacy and flight. Rain washed them out,
but you made others. Toward the end of May
I thought I was turning into you; I would wake at night
to touch breasts and the long, polished
legs, the brief pubis,
imagining, maybe becoming, maybe being,
the frightened and dumbfounded
inhabiter of your body. My mouth formed words,
but it was you who spoke, you
who turned with flour to your elbows, a streak
of white curving across your forehead, you
who stood in the wind
calling our dog with names
that didn't belong to him, or to me.

Cycles

I think it is well known now
how you can take one part of the country
and re-erect it somewhere else, how the abrupt, snow-streaked
mountains of New Mexico hang in a dark corner
of your uncle's hall. And some morning in late winter
the trees are diadems of ice,
the way they were once, miraculously, on the river in Florida,
when you were a child. It is not
that we wish the courage
to ask a co-worker
for the loan of her beach house, it is not
that. Or the madwoman,
slick with terror and grease, interrupting mass—
that something in here
would take hold suddenly, and calm her. O the priests
do their duty
because they are pros. And the world
was always crumbling fast; it is not that we wish the world
other than it is. My friend asks
what's your hurry? we are all headed
to the grave. Only, I guess,
I seek a certain rhythm, the dumb bob
of a pigeon's head, the old friend
calling from Kansas, the muck of love—
its resignation and exuberance—the red flowers
returned to the trees
as if winter was nothing to them, nothing at all.

Now I Smack My Head

I've taken too many things seriously,
for example: that there is inherent
seriousness in everything,
if we can just locate it, it being
our duty to try. Now I smack my head
and cry *How could I have been so stupid—*
the rain is only the rain, my
boy. But then I am coming out of the library, late,
after watching Laurel and Hardy
in *Sons of the Desert*, and already I can't stop
thinking of Oliver Hardy's face,
the four thousand expressions, from horror
to smirkery, that pass over it
as he waits for his wife
to let him have it, and rain is dripping
from the aged ginkgo dumbly springing its leaves
again, there is the smell
of pizza dough, a wet dog crosses the street,
and I can't do anything
for about ten seconds but stand there
with my heart pounding wildly,
seriously in love with it all.

The Meaning of Birds

Of the genesis of birds we know nothing,
save the legend they are descended
from reptiles: flying, snap-jawed lizards
that have somehow taken to air. Better the story
that they were crabapple blossoms
or such, blown along by the wind; time after time
finding themselves tossed from perhaps a seaside tree,
floated or lifted over the thin blue lazarine waves
until something in the snatch of color
began to flutter and rise. But what does it matter
anyway how they got up high
in the trees or over the rusty shoulders
of some mountain? There they are,
little figments,
animated—soaring. And if occasionally a tern washes up
greased and stiff, and sometimes a cardinal
or a mockingbird slams against the windshield
and your soul goes *oh God* and shivers
at the quick and unexpected end
to beauty, it is not news that we live in a world
where beauty is unexplainable
and suddenly ruined
and has its own routines. We are often far
from home in a dark town, and our griefs
are difficult to translate into a language
understood by others. We sense the downswing of time
and learn, having come of age, that the reluctant
concessions made in youth
are not sufficient to heat the cold drawn breath
of age. Perhaps temperance
was not enough, foresight or even wisdom
fallacious, not only in conception
but in the thin acts

themselves. So our lives are difficult,
and perhaps unpardonable, and the fey gauds
of youth have, as the old men told us they would,
faded. But still, it is morning again, this day.
In the flowering trees
the birds take up their indifferent, elegant cries.
Look around. Perhaps it isn't too late
to make a fool of yourself again. Perhaps it isn't too late
to flap your arms and cry out, to give
one more cracked rendition of your singular, aspirant song.

Respite

Someone walking in the western dust
says *Our lives*
are not ours to take away,
and I am immensely relieved by this, I think
it means we can get on with whatever haphazard
project we've signed
on to do, whether it's my brother's
scheme to move the red sandstone
mountain off his homestead
in Utah, or that painter,
the aborigine I met three
years ago, who was the last one who knew
the ancient designs he painted from root
and jackflower dye onto bark,
and was so solemn and so solemnly
happy about it—happy the way we were happy,
making love all afternoon, as finally the rain
broke through the heat wave,
and we watched the ivy
on the next building gather the silver droplets,
and the shouts from the street
became muted,
almost tender, as above the city
lightning flashed
and the suicides climbed down from the roofs.

from THE PALMS

This Holy Enterprise

The troubled entrepreneurs of evening—
the palm readers, the Mexican bracelet salesmen,
the girl who dances on a sheet of tin—
call out to me, turning for one second
their voices into instruments of love and attention,
promising love and attention, the Grail
of whatever singular prize I have longed for
and now found. I honor them all,
as I honor the priests
and the women who scream at the rain,
as I honor the envelope of bills and silver change
the boss hands me on Saturdays
saying *This is my body.* I have come around
to a pure absolution, gained—like a handful of grain
from the lords—by obedience, so that if I lie
all day Sunday like an effigy of myself,
harmless on the bed,
listening to the rants and vows
rising from the street, it is not because
I consider myself grandee of a greater enterprise,
but a child who listens at the door of his parents' room,
spellbound by the explanations they offer each other
of why the world moves
like a brutish uncle, drunk, through the house.
It is a tone I listen for, an inflection,
the moment when the argument breaks down
because someone can't take it anymore.

The Woman as Figure

Why, when I see the child
walking with the woman at a little distance
from the blowing trees, see the pale blue figures
of the fog, and the patches of light like just-opened
passages on the sea, does my mind veer
to violence, why then do I think something terrible
is about to happen, and why do I think the woman
has known this all along, and is waiting for it to begin,
the blows and the harsh breathing and the cries
of accusation and helplessness? I think
I am being used by something violent and merciless,
and I can't think of a way to make
this perception believable or pertinent, the way the woman,
entering a church to get out of the rain,
will shake the water from her hair
and look around her at the ornately extruded display,
the tons of bullion, to find a point of simplicity,
maybe the embroidered hem, maybe the soft curve
of a saint's elbow, maybe the single sliver of bluish light
falling across the back of a man knelt
praying, and take this into herself,
as one would take a small piece of treasure
offered in passing by a king, who himself,
worried and overcome by the problems of the state,
dreams of a garden, the one he knew as a child,
where he walked among the long hesitations of twilight,
planning battles and gaily painted ships
on fire and death sentences only he could rescind.

The Palms

When the sun went down in L.A. that day I was driving
a rental car east on Sunset Boulevard,
worn down by the endless internal battering,
and looked back to see the vivid capacious burned oceanic light,
the dust in the air that made the light palpable and beautiful
hanging over the pastel city, and saw the crunched little stores
with their brocades of steel locking them up
and the narrow streets springing downhill like madmen
running away; and there was a ridge that blocked the sun,
a scruffy torn wall of yellow earth with a few small houses on top,
widely spaced, disconnected-looking, though down from them
there was a neighborhood of bunched-up shacks
and a street that wound through patches of willow and bougainvillea;
and on the ridge that was sharply defined by the
rotted unmanageable light, there were a few palm trees,
untouched at that moment by breeze so that their tops
hung limply; and they seemed, black against the huge sky
of Los Angeles, like small dark thoughts tethered
at the end of reason's thick ropes, hanging there in gratuitous solitude,
like the thoughts of a man behind a cluttered restaurant counter,
who speaks no English, wearing a hat made of butcher paper,
who slaps and slaps his small daughter, until they both are stunned,
stupid and helpless, overwhelmed by their lives.

Omnipotence

I wanted to see the emotion in my brother's face
the night his child was born, I wanted tears, the face
red and beaten and his wife gray and nearly dead
in the ripped sheets and the baby slick
from the gushed oils of the body—I was glad my brother
couldn't take the birth and ran outside
to vomit into the gardenias and the midwife ordered
him to stay there and his wife screamed and choked
and screamed for help and my brother fell to his knees
in the yard praying or crying and the storm whipped
the chinaberries and made the fence wire sing and
the old house thumped and thudded against itself
as the crying and the screaming went on until
dawn when as the gray streaks raised themselves
like Hercules lifting the night off I saw
the ground littered with blue flowers and my brother
soaked to the skin slumped against the side of the house
while the midwife, tense on the steps, looked down at him
holding herself in bloody arms apologizing.

Redneck Riviera

We ate at a poor restaurant
that was brightly lit and where the waitress
who was new at the job
tried hard to get our orders right
and brought a piece of streaky fish
that was tough and tasteless while around us
sunburned families from country towns in Alabama
and south Georgia ate the same food
without saying much
to the waitress or each other.
It was such a starry night
and we were such a long way from home,
still so shaky with each other
after the scare of our marriage falling
apart, that I leaned over and kissed
you on the mouth and tasted the lemon
and the dry baked fish
like ashes on the lips of the dead.

Mother at Eighty

You come in dream, Mother, or not at all,
distressed by drugs, scattering quips, complaining
still about the way they torture you. Married late,
you wouldn't leave the party, forced Hawaii
to its knees; I've seen the cascades of your hair,
heard the devilish laugh each suitor ducked, ricocheting
through the rooms; a wastrel girl, uncontrollable.
And press through time to take you in my arms,
to find you now, coldcocked by suffering,
baggage in a train that's plowed its way
into the dark and snowy woods, and stopped.
I see you there, my dreamer, nodding at your window,
unacknowledged, except perhaps by the spotted dog
limping in the snow, that sees you lift your head,
and trembles in your smoky, avid glance.

The Rose

I'm looking everywhere for new ways,
poking, selecting, looking everywhere,
turning the trees over, rummaging among skirts
and stars. I'm so lonely and intense, so
tense and energetic, I'm getting up early
to touch the slick habit of ice on the windowsill,
to touch dust and the dried blue berries of juniper.
I'm shaking and scared of life
and of the absence of life, childless, love
buried out in the prairie far from here
under the shifty grass; I'm watching the white birds
drift up from the south, reading the last lights
in the tall buildings like lines of white type
spelling the future, I'm into everything
haphazardly and wholly, revenant and pilgrim,
I'm looking as I go and I go formally and
rapidly, moving through gales of solitude,
through crowds and the cries of young children;
I'm tasting, I'm smelling everything, I'm
stooping in Chinatown to kiss the boots of
the Buddhists, I'm pressing my bare skin
to the ancient stone designs of artisans lost
to the world; I'm looking everywhere, I'm alert,
I'm open like a child's blue coat as he runs,
I'm ready for bronze and happiness, I'm gamely
adjusting the water level, I'm forgiving it all,
telling it all, hearing it all, I'm ready
for fake silk patches spilling from envelopes,
I'm ready for a "vague splintering of rain,"
ready—I'm looking everywhere—for a delicate
means of transition, I'm stumbling against
beauty and not apologizing, I'm almost naked here,
skinnier than I used to be, almost helpless

or maybe I'm completely helpless as the religious
say is the way to heaven—all right I'm helpless—
I'm swaying on the platform, I'm tenderly
toasting the bread, I'm placing the saucer,
the spoon on the tray, I'm arranging the rose,
I'm pulling the curtain, I'm letting light flood the room.

from BEFORE AND AFTER

The Sentinel

Around the family my brother's sure of himself,
he doesn't want advice, extra love, he's sown
his life right up to the doorstep and knows
it prospers, he can look out the window and see
how well he's done, nobody has to tell him,
nobody can accuse him of failure. I'm always
a little dizzy in his house, a little lost
and indecisive, I let his daughters kiss me
and make me play odd complicated games they make up
that go on endlessly until we are so tired we
want to fall asleep on the floor. My brother's always
fixing things, always planning, he scrapes the rust
off a hinge, gets down on his knees and looks
into the crawl space for what's rotten down there,
finds it and gouges it out while his daughters
win again at their indecipherable games; his wife
sits in the kitchen looking around, she gave up
a career for this, she barks and complains
in the empty kitchen as the night stands up close
against the windows like big hands covering her eyes,
she has counted to a hundred and is about to get up
and put a stop to something, somewhere, in some house.

Defiance

I go through periods, a grown man, still reluctant
to talk to my father, I let him call and leave messages
while I sit there like a fox in the woods waiting.
I don't answer, I don't say anything, I let the night
and the thick woods of my anger enclose me, I feel
the whole side of the country curled up around me,
the freshness of the faraway streams, the naked rocks,
the jitter and hiss of smaller animals
earnestly going about their business, as my business
sinks to its essential breath and heartbeat until
I am so quiet you'd have to be connected to me by blood
to know I hadn't died there squatting with my eyes open,
and even then you couldn't be sure.

Ruffians

When my father got old, but not too old,
his body went bad, fantastically crumpled,
not like the body of a man who'd spent his life making business,
but like a logger's or a rodeo rider's,
and then only if these men had kept at it,
hacked and rode into their sixties
until the feet, the spine, the heart gave way,
until you found them flat out under a plastic shell,
ripped chest sewn up with stitches thick as the rings
in a child's notebook, until, when the machines had pumped breath
and even life back, you found them propped dizzy in bed
held upright by a brace like a lobster's thorax,
legs shriveled, hair white on every part of the body;
and they never shed a tear, these ruffians,
so even you, the persistent son,
who hated the clink of spurs, the ring of an ax, were moved,
until you could see how hard it was to break a man,
and how sometimes the worst changes nothing,
as if this were a world where knowledge, forbearance,
the whole process of improvement and surrender didn't matter,
and life itself, come in at nightfall from the rainy fields,
stood on the threshold looking at you, without recognition.

The Business

My father and his brother didn't get along;
for years they kept at it, sniping, digging
out the ground under each other's feet;
it was a life work more important
than family, than community. My grandfather
set them to it, yoked them
into his business, struck one against the other
to make sparks, raise a fire that would warm him.

My grandfather was a brilliant man;
he knew what a son will do for a father's love,
how success is a knife driven into the brother's chest,
how one must pay with another's life
for his own; he knew
what a sure thing it was, this jealousy,
like a magic bread
that doesn't run out,
that will feed a man as long as he lives.

The Essential Story

We each wanted our own story, my father and I;
we were talkers, him first then me,
each wanted the other to listen until his heart broke.
It didn't matter where the story began,
or what it was about, each had a better one,
each had gone out farther, seen more,
each needed—this time—to be listened to;
each was ready to kill the other to get him to shut up.

Or so it seemed to me
until I hated him. He had the advantage,
years when I didn't exist; he knew war, marriage,
the birth of sons, decline; I knew dreams, agility,
desire, a boy's demands. It was no wonder I got out of there,
no wonder I ran for my life.

Everywhere I went, sons out on bail
yapped like maniacs. And every time a man stopped me
to pour out his heart, I understood why he did this.
And the whispers in theaters,
and the soft patter after lovemaking,
and the derelict explaining himself to a building
—I understood. A boy can't make his father listen,
and he can't make his father stop talking.
Even years later, when I returned,
my father wouldn't let me get a word in,
he had so much to say about how he missed me.

Conceit

My brother's afraid to get angry,
he's terrified of what'll happen. I disappoint him
and he writes a lightly chiding
letter you have to be related to him to know
is cut from a block of solid rage.
He's afraid if he makes the slightest move,
wants the window open
instead of shut, disagrees, he'll provoke
a demon who'll destroy us all.

It's one of those situations
you never get used to, but can't change:
the end jostling the middle,
interrupting the beginning,
until whichever way you look
the worst is always there.

In my family we're all missing something,
something beautiful we once saw,
like a yellow carriage disappearing over a hill;
we were—so we believed—
supposed to follow, join the jolly company.
But this is only speculation.
We don't talk about what we missed.
We write letters filled with praise
and crossed-out words like scars in flesh.

There Is No Railroad Named Delight

My great-aunt, a diabetic
and selfish woman, killed herself with fudge.
She'd had enough of being good.
Got up at three, went downstairs,
and poisoned herself with sugar.

I don't think she meant to die. I think
she couldn't wait another minute
for her pleasure in this world.
Selfish yes, but this, a need that drives us
to the grave in fits of passion
and excess, stands for something else.

We're ravenous all right—you see it every day—
and can't refuse the stroke
we step into like a child into a sprinkler's
bristly fan. Inside, for some,
it's dark and cramped all the time.
And nothing in the world of standard means
can air the murky vaults. You know how it starts:
upright in church, it's spring,
a softened, gentle breeze drifts in,
you turn your head, see your child
caught inside a beam of yellow light,
and feel the kick of death.

Anticipation

I think he ought to practice,
but he won't; he ought to get used to things.
It's death, I say; get ready.
But he goes on talking about life.
He liked it here, he had a good time.
You would too, he says, if you'd relax.
I can't, I tell him, this is too much for me.
For me too, he says, but so what. He's not dead yet.
I've lived by pretending what's coming
is already here. I said my wife was gone
months before she left. Anticipation—for me
that was the key. But he goes on eating peaches,
planning for spring, hooking the holes of his life
to the cleats of the future. It won't come,
everyone can see this. Death's
taking over the property. I look up,
and the sky's a huge blueprint
for an estate about to be built,
and I don't know the first thing about hammers
or nails. I roll him to the window
so he can see, but to him the sky is delight,
and the clouds are just puffs and white china dogs.

The Miniature City

The aging family life fades out, subsides,
but it is only a diminution, a reduction in scale,
like a city reduced to miniature,
archival, but still functioning, its nubby trees,
groans, the flared soft words of love,
boys running with their coats burst wide,
still the same as ever, all proportion,
whimsy, what looks fatal in the face of one
you've known since you were young, still the same;

even blunted rage
lodged beneath the skin,
the screams that faded out years ago,
leak their future into lives just now coming up the street,
and the tiny shouts of children
in a distance that began when you were born,
though faint, are clear, every baffled claim
still unresolved, and the same with grief,
like a perfect wound, that aches but doesn't show.

from HEROIN AND OTHER POEMS

Real Time

. . . where Hiroshima was, someone said, there's a little star,
and I saw this star, like spit on the sidewalk
. . . and there's a quiet inlet of oaks,
someone said, a brazen light,
and a perpetual return, another promised,
and someone was always having a bad time of it,
grim forecasts and the heart worn down,
punched-in shops on the highway where we bought beer,
and that spring we argued all night,
night after night, and couldn't save the marriage—all that
someone said, will be replaced,
like a city replaced by a meadow
and replaced by a city again—and the little shudder
I got thinking of absent time,
or time without us in it,
and how, sometimes, a friend said, any thought of another
is godlike, is grace, and I read somewhere
about how tired explorers get just before they reach the goal,
about various seaweeds, movies shown in the open air,
about a river pressing in among the trees, and someone said
we all wish to publish manifestos,
and in the decline of summer that year
translations of old ideas appeared like new,
and someone nearly hysterical claimed
he never heard the announcement, and couldn't get out of the way.

Louisiana Purchase

Who knows but that Meriwether Lewis's
lost diaries might turn up yet
packed in a can in some cramped ex-midden
dug up a thousand years from now,
that elegant, exfoliate style
continue on up the Missouri, into sadness
and disrepute, the suicide in a hotel in Tennessee
no more important now than the bundle
of grasses my friend made out in the woods
yesterday and gave to me after a meeting
in which she confessed she's afraid of everything
that's coming. The past I don't mind, she said,
and laughed as if that was something.

The World as Will and Representation

... *dissatisfied egotistical state*: Schopenhauer's way of putting things,
thinking about us:
                    we are terribly agitated, he says,
no hope for us in good works, or in facts,
            no treehouses or illuminated backyard fetes, no
                        investigations carried on under duress
or played-out hunches described in late-night diners
four hours outside Las Vegas,
will do the trick.

Unable to free ourselves from guilt (we're born guilty)
            our only chance an extreme form of asceticism (quietism, button-upism),
lie low in other words, shake off will and desire, no demands.
                    Yet, without the framing of a larger hope, a structure
            that sustains and relieves the pressure of humanness, I wonder
how this is possible.

                    S okays art (the experience of art
constitutes cessation of the will:
                        beauty wipes the slate clean),
but what about sports or galloping a horse through a field of lupine,
or reading your long-dead unmarried aunt's mail
                        and speculating about "Roberto,"
wondering why she described the days as "voluminous and without delight,"

or the first time you bought reefer,
                    or taking the limousine back from a Yankees game,
stopping off for steaks at Frank's on Little West 12th
and seeing some gorgeous woman
get out of a cab and realizing this is your wife?

what of love?

what of tempestuousness and what of tumult,
what of the irresolution of nights on backporches as love spirals down
all around you,

the bare times of scorn and vituperation,

the losses, the brief asides in which we fill our minds with the glorious mischances
and duplications of someone else's life, where would
we be (unquiet, fractious) without
these maddening disagreements, men putting things badly,
women addressing the wrong party, junkyards of rust
and dereliction reminding us of our fallibility, the fallibility itself
and the remorse that push us to do better next time,

and what of desire
almost endless,

and appetite and loss of control

what of
wayward indiscreet possessiveness under big trees in Miami,
or some such place,
her fingers smelling of Cuban spices,
and the way
she turned to say
she couldn't go on without a kiss?

The idea, he says, is to remove us from time.

Life, according to S, is suffering
and death is its promised land.

What's left is the inner life, salients
and extended peregrinations and long afternoons muttering of conspiracies,
random phrases circulating among the back precincts of thought,

confused ramblings passing as speculation,

        and speculation itself, the grand moment when
some obscure principle too difficult to repeat or revise begins to make sense, sure,
philosophical systems ground into powder and blown into the eyes of children,

reveries in which we come to understand that true idealism,

           as S says, "is not the empirical,

                but the transcendental."

    "The world is my representation," he says.

I want to be comforted.

I want to leave the house without worrying about what I left
or left unfinished there.

         Nature, S points out,
accepts us back to its bosom, dead,
without comment.

He means death's not the big deal, we're coming home.

What I mean is I want something to be so true I forget it
and go on fully absorbed out on the dock where the ocean lifts and
falls back sighing.

I notice the gold
streaks on a woman's arm,
the boys boxing under the pines.

Straight

In all these old photographs sun
shines directly into every face;
it's a rule and makes the past seem
brightly lit, a world exposed and
direct, shadows only in the back,
behind things; and each of them,
men and women once young who are
dead now, children risen from curls
into heavy labor and troubled sleep,
accept this effortlessly; their bodies
look like shields, their faces shine,
and their eyes, looking straight at you,
hold sunlight off like an army; even
pale loitering boys and girls without
charm, women already oppressed beyond
endurance, the big father sprouting
hair on his arms like brushed wire,
in frank sunlight they do not shrink
from, appear touched by a familiar
eternity they don't dream will fail.

Los Dos Rancheros

I can see the moon like a bullet sunk in the clouds' body
and it seems to me the worst has happened. *Nothing*
really touches me, she says, and begins to express her contempt.
For a second everything gets transparent. At my cafe breakfast
I sweat profusely and attempt to comfort
the silverware and consider the water, shimmering
in its glass like precious liquid crystal, to be my friend.
When the government cars go by, the big black-curtained cars
containing dignitaries who will one day beg God to save them,
I get up from my seat and stand on the steps looking at the sky
trying not to think of how what was between us—whatever
you call this corybantic—turned up dead this morning,
but it's no use. Now everything refers to it,
including the young man in the Los Dos Rancheros Restaurant
dreaming Puebla or Ixtlán back into shape, who
jabs one song after another into the jukebox
hard like a man jabbing his finger into the face
of someone impossible to convince, who halfway to his table
stops to throw his head back and laugh with a sound
like a grease fire smothering. I walk out into the
charmlessly evincerating street
where everyone is doing the best he can to keep the dark
from climbing over his back. *Take your hands off me*,
a woman screams and throws herself out of a car.
Even in sleep, the blind newsdealer says, *my life is confusion*.
From here I plot a course that will take me into an area
in which I am respected and praised for leaving her.
You can look me up, she's saying into the phone when I return,
I am the one who fell in love with the captain and lost her honor
not to mention her fortune and now I live
this retired life, that is to say this life of routine
and memory in which I am without hope. Says this
and gives me a look. Quietly the strangulations begin again.
What do you think? That nothing can kill the world, not even love?

Honesty

Maybe Anna won't arrive.
Maybe mordant self-concern will become love.
O you who know things
never change. I imagine
E. A. Poe kissing his child bride, thirteen-year-old girl
her mother standing in for his mother
sweet-tempered raking roast potatoes from the fire,
and shiver with tension and morbidity.
He was appalled by loneliness
by scary apartness, shuddering with resentment
and an alarming sense of smothering.
He lived a while in a bee glade,
high on the island, in NYC.
Anna is
Anna Karenina. Maybe
she won't reach the station.
I used to think the fact my
crazy mother was still alive
meant there was hope. A fool's notion.
She became unreachable
long ago.
In the untidy Southern village I come from
this is not unusual.
People are set.
Vietnam was so great, my friend says,
because folks who would never
get a chance to change their minds, did.
Like my friend's father fat ex-Air Force sergeant
who at last, weeping at the grave,
cried Please God end this, it's no good.
Not the *end this* important, but the *it's no good.*
A change of heart.
Not Vronsky saying okay

I didn't mean it, forget the war,
I love you let's get married raise a family,
but Anna.
It's no good. And Edgar Poe,
this weeping into my hat, tugging the sleeve
of a dead child-woman: It's no good.

Once in my junkie days I kept a cattle herd.
It was winter in the mountains,
prohibitive, rage like a canvas shirt caked in ice,
I pushed hay bales out of a truck.
The cows, fretful women,
their bony hips, moaning, snotty,
when they snuffled up
I'd punch them in the face.
I wanted to punch
my wife
and the side of the mountain
and my life snarled like a deer in a fence.
I was filled with longing
for joyful permanent fixations, and insight,
for play and a secular individualism,
a spiritual life and some unnameable
opportunity like a right I vaguely
remembered and couldn't get purchase on.
It was no good.
It took me years and one mistake
after another to realize this
and even then I simply got washed out,
put aside
I didn't really learn a lesson.
I know it's not so much the mistakes
not the divisions, or cultural impediments,
the threats and isolation techniques
we run on each other

it's the heart.
My father went to his grave unchanged.
So did Poe.
And beautiful Anna Karenina.
And Ovid. Consuela Concepción, too, my piano teacher.
They say in the end
Mussolini was so terrified his mind seized and he couldn't speak.
He sat there swelled-up and bug-eyed. This is not it.
Or anyone drowning or
lurching from the fire shrieking he didn't want this to happen.
There is so much gibberish. And imprecision.
No wonder we lock in.
Like you, I get scared.
I used to go to my friend's house,
sink into the old sofa on his backporch
and read all day. His family
and the ducks and dogs would pass by,
let me be—discreet love—I'd feel safe.
It was just after I stumbled out of my second marriage.
My friend practiced a religion
remarkable in its narrow-mindedness. He inserted
his children into this olla podrida
like a man stuffing leaves into a shoe.
It hurt to see it.
Broken saddle bronc of a beautiful face he had
and his wife a slim twist of blonde girl cunning
and fretful without shame
about anything—I spoke up eventually and got tossed.

I've spent years watching television.
I lie on the couch
eating chocolate and watching television,
arguing with some woman in my head.
Television says the world is not a mysterious place.
Don't worry, it says,

you don't have to change a thing.
And then I remember digging wild leeks,
buying eggs from a crippled old lady
who glanced into the next room sadly
as if a great novelist was dying in there,
and went on
talking, like Kissinger after the war.
And how scary things became when my wife
got up close. Change of heart.
Love leeching the lining away, exposing the pulp.
Stupidity and malice
and a fitful generosity,
shortsightedness and painful posturing,
and things continue just as they are,
nutcases, disputes,
overbearing stupid
claims, modernity hamming it up,
life someone says only a device for entering other realms
—all these in the hopper.
And the tough decisions.
Poe dreaming of a cold finger
picking the lock. Anna stuffing screams back down.
Let go, or stay with it?
The Dalai Lama saying *Sure, sure, I'll take the sprouts,*
including the Chinese in everything.
My girlfriend stunned by the power of her own rage,
nothing she can do about it yet,
rebuking paradise, groping for the cat.

Family Burial

All around water moves, rocking . . .
    slide of river, current a snake descending the tree,
        meets the tide returning after a night in the
        wilderness . . .
men reveal themselves only with great reluctance,
take years to tell a friend,
change of heart that for some comes snapped upright
and smoldering for others appears gradually
over years so slowly nothing's different, we recall
another arrangement perhaps, candles the color of sunshine,
a small basket of silver rings, tall columns of amber light
    love slipped through . . .
        not until Father died, the river says, did I know I
        could live.

Beds

Terrible beds, soft beds, wily, elusive beds,
beds of half-grown boys, fey and trembling,
    dumped on their ear beds of traveling salesmen surprised,
girl beds and virginal young woman beds,
    matronal expansively expressed beds, I think of these,
recalled to sleep, out of sleep into sleep,
    waked early, waked late at night remembering,
drunken beds, sopping watery beds, pissed-in beds,
    beds come to me, all I have slept in,
beds I have knelt beside and dreamed of,
    bench one foot wide for a bed in Saipan,
hay barn in Turkey bed, dawn like sherbet
    naked men stood up out of, trickling weedy beds,
greetings and good-byes from beds,
    sullen, imperious beds . . . there was always a bed,
place to lie down, if only for a pause, in jail
    or in the aisle of a bus, berths belowdecks
diesel smoke and topside typhoon,
    Pacific swells, trough and deep-six beds for lost sailors,
mountain beds often cold and wet,
    sooty nights risen from bed drunk
whirling in the yard lie abed in grass
    or among tomato vines and springy corn
love gone from my bed
    love lost to another's, searching the cold
fabrications for clues, bed stains
    and scented sheets, beds of humiliation
and scorn, shivering clothed in unheat until dawn
    friend appearing through white cloud said
Go now to the neighbors . . . hot bath like a bed,
    and beds of fern and moss
and pine boughs, beds in Istanbul Hotel plush
    and beds in Florence and golden Madrid,

Southern beds and beds in New England tucked under quilts,
     cornfed beds and *lit de cassis*, and narrow bed of devotion,
bed of love, of endurance,
     bed of turmoil and surrender
and change slow to come,
     bed of low spoken phrases,
bed of form become style
     bed of California grape arbors
and outdoor beds and beds on porches
     and beds in back bedrooms where the crazy son died
beds in attics and in upper stories down long stone corridors
     beds that trembled and bunk beds
and beds without meaning
     beds in trees,
in grass, in fields of clover
     beds in fragrant lover's arms,
beds multiplied into
     nights sleepless and disordered in beds,
into nights of confusion and dismay,
     of lust
of hatred and pride mixed in a sour beam
     of persistence, nights of fear,
nights of memory
     and applicable recall,
nights of kisses, nights of frankness
     passing for truth, nights of delightful smells,
nights on the river, by the sea, inland nights
     spoken of in hushed voices, nights by the wayside,
nights come to bed late for no reason,
     nights spent for a time sitting on the bathroom floor,
nights and days and the next night in bed
     recovering from serious illness, in beds without exits,
beds stepped boldly up to, beds
     unfolding like mysteries, childhood beds,
the beds of adulthood and youth,

Chinese beds, decent Norwegian beds,
Filipino tropical beds,
   stained beds, beds soaked in perfume, striped
and checkered beds, all night spent
   beside someone's bed, beside beds of loved ones,
the bed my father died in burned the next day
   in a pit behind the house, my mother's bed empty
for years, beds of my wives, beds of children
   raised from their beds and sent forth into the world,
soft and ample and undivided beds,
   nights lingering quietly in the mind,
beds you spoke of as we lay after supper calm in our bed
   listening to night come down around us,
settled and consonant, happy in our bed.

Calling for Clare

I survey my manuscripts for flaws in judgment,
for some hint of what I might really mean,
and then, unsatisfied by this,
I lie in the dark, the semidark,
listening to the airwaves,
listening for something familiar,
some exclusive.
I know my hands smell of reproach
and humiliation,
and it is no leap to admit
I have begun to apologize to buildings and whole districts,
to trees and to the people standing under them,
but still I am afraid I have missed something crucial,
some valid point,
in my dead brother's phrase,
that entered the discussion a while back
and changed everything.
I have cultivated an approach
obviously out of step with my peers, but I can't stop now.
I mean I have stopped now.
We could go into my room if you like
and discuss absence.
A number of important concepts and entities
are missing.
We might press an ear to the wall
and listen to next door's desperate case. He's sobbing again
and calling for Clare.
Afterwards we can taunt ourselves
with near misses.
Recently someone—I swear it's not me—
was seen crawling along a darkened corridor.
I myself was fired,
so I'm told, from various jobs

I never applied for, or held.
Someone else is picking up
my check. And D's in my thoughts again,
somehow she's
found her way back there.
My thoughts of Maine
and its coarse conifery and moose habitat,
its unsolved mysteries and streets emptied by rain.

As for Trees

. . . there are the stupendous oaks and hickories I climbed,
catafalques and monuments, broken-down harassed improvident trees,
unconnected, poorly constructed unsought-after trees, there are bundled sticks,

shaken willows, river birches without footings and over-investigated,
dramatized firs, celibate, virginal pines, capacious elms,
birches divided against themselves, groves come up short, repudiated locusts,

there are maples and obvious sycamores, poplars slender as tax collectors,
duplicated laurels, chinaberry, redwoods without scruples, divisive, whining persimmons,
trees of legend and saplings writhing as if on fire,

                         there are saucy, duplicitous conifers,

everyday live oaks, trees with limbs like thighs, like torsos, like dolphins
rotting on a dock, trees made of deerhide and pleurisy, trees without meaning
beyond the noise they make, there are sumac and buckeye and hawthorn of the rose family,

there's mulberry my girlfriend eats of, there is a tree
with no name, there are druidical subversive trees, trees the old man
thinks of when he walks around at night whistling,

                       there is Sherwood Forest and

delayed reactions taking place under trees,

                       there is a large following

for some trees, flower and fruit, there are roots poking from the ground,
there is the holly & the effervescent plum, bamboo, lignum vitae, crabapple, chokecherry & bay,

there are the trees I have slept under, trees lightning loves, luxurious undulant trees,
immaculate trees and dogwoods forlorn and white-headed in the spring woods,
there are trees in various locales unthought of, trees at the dump and camphor trees

in graveyards & companionable junipers & redbuds & Japanese magnolias and crepe myrtle &
dahoon, tupelo, viburnum, spruce, catalpa and gum,

there are loquacious trees

and trees that fidget and trees that seem to move around at night,
and voices coming from trees and the famous cedars of Lebanon,

and there are the inveterate hustlers, the trees with red berries and there are
trees like Italian laughter, and unbedded trees, and pepper trees and trees by the ocean
and beeches behind the dunes,

there's rhododendron and laurel, basswood and hop hornbeam

there's yucca and coral tree,

eternal trees and golden trees and trees sewn up tight
and undetectable trees and cautious, dependable trees, and there are fruits
fallen close to the tree and accidents of birth, and trees like hogs run through,

and there is the tree I kissed my first wife under
and the tree she remembered and her red-stained mouth,

there is my friend buried under a myrtle tree, and there's the sand hickory
and the pecan and the raccoon in the loblolly pine, and there are the laurel, black haw, cherry
and mountain ash and the box elder torn down by hurricane,

there're more trees in the Smokies than anywhere else, there are
trees colossal in their own minds,
sacrificed trees, stumps and root systems upended on ranches,

there is hemlock and silver bell and sparkleberry and peach,
mimosas come to mind, and the obvious silk tree, I saw a tamarack once,
and at the botanical gardens there are banyan trees and baobabs and a cypress

like the cypress

on Christopher Street,

there are locust pods like arched black eyebrows of amazed seigneurs,
and there are the brittle limbs of the London plane tree,

there are simple quivering trees and foxhaven trees and there's a tree
in the middle of my second wife's living room,

there is sassafras, yaupon and pear, there are trees we all love,
cottonwoods and the fragile chestnut, doomed to die, trees that linger
like Spanish perfume,

        and there are trees getting things together finally
and trees marshaling their forces and there are trees without hope,
losers and touts down on their luck

        and there's an ailanthus behind the
Jesu Christo Es El Señor Liquor Store, a spindly tree, smoke-bit and softened up
by winter, a tree we could go without noticing, and in sooty backyards

there are flowering fruit trees and there's buckthorn and fig, codicils
and allusions to trees and the brief aside once about a tree in the mind,
African and European trees, walnut trees and butternut, hapless trees once human,

there's a rumor about trees and someone mutters like a tree muttering to the wind,

there are corolla, calyx and sepals, red-bit or yellow, white as a sheet falling,

we distinguish various shapes for leaves, the round and the spearlike lance, the
egg-shaped and the frog-footed, the simple leaves of chokecherry and sourwood droop in
summer, juniper leaves threadlike or stiff & bony, needles blunted,
        hugging the ground in winter,

there are leaves euphonious, sighing leaves, whistling, soughing, moaning leaves,
whole boughs moving as if about to exit the earth, rattling of palms,
clatter of magnolias, radiant buckeye leaves as if offering five paths,

there are the meaningless confidential remarks, the questing of pines, forthright pistachios,
the obstinate oaks, the complicated stirring of the honey locust,
there are catkins and bouquets, single florets dipped in wax,

spatters of scarlet in the white, vague yellow musings, blue silk bits,
rouged lip skin peeled off and crumpled up,

                                        there are

calcified leaves and flowers without distinction and strings of yellow
in late spring, and bunches and unstrung wreaths, stalks of red and yellow,
creamy blisterings, there are petals in her hair,

there are acorns and multitudes of purple berries and illiterate pignuts and prickly filberts,
buckeyes and tufted sycamore balls, various pods, peas of all sizes, tough horned pellets
and sheaths discarded, husks and hulls, burst maple cases

                                        and the shredded dresses of virginal alders,
carelessly tossed aside, coats and leggings, shoes, slippers, scabbards, and smashed violins,
there are the round red berries of the possum haw,

and the splashy, lyric fruits,
I could mention these, epic groves,
fall rattling up its ladders to set fire in the trees.

The Trail

In cities you never visited I sensed your presence.
In bungalow colonies and airport delicatessens

I caught sight of someone
who might have been you, but I couldn't catch up.

I rented apartments and left them vacant in hopes
you might appear, like a vision.

In Utah, a ridgeline seemed to be leading toward you,
but I was wrong.

I tried each highway, driving slowly
so as not to miss you if you'd pulled over to rest.

I descended into coastal cities, often at dawn,
and sat in coffee shops waiting for you.

In hotel rooms
I watched for the phone's blinking light.

I tried to be precise, and maintain confidence,
repeating supportive phrases from my reading,

attempting to stay calm, but often I fell to pieces.
I encountered conscripts and justifiers like myself,

apparitions shouting their news into traffic,
but nothing they told me touched on you.

I eavesdropped on conversations, listening
for the choked-down sobs of the grief-stricken.

Up on the mesa, by a motel pool, I read a story out loud,
a tale in which the author wrote eloquently

of the queerly resolute heroine's
quiet life in a cabin by a meadow,

where the fall, still cordial to its summer,
had begun to streak the poplars faintly gold.

Even then—and I tried hard—
I couldn't picture you.

Indians Driving Pickup Trucks

I have this complicated friend who teaches poetry at H—.
She takes time off regularly and drives nonstop
to New Mexico where she sets up in an old adobe
and furiously writes stories about women thumbing rides
through the desert, women who climb in with Indians
driving pickup trucks, are taken back to the rez for treatment,
love treatment and such, and then spend years out there
with their hair in a twist, raking in the yard.

She loves this material and hates her life, she says.
Each day, she says, *is like a door I plunge out of, on fire.*
You wouldn't believe what goes on under this breastbone.
And hits her chest with a thumb knuckle.

She cleans everything out of the house and
then sits on the floor writing into a blue notebook.
It's an entirely empty house, two rooms—in New Mexico—
up on the mesa, under a strict blue sky.
Outside men in pickup trucks throw beer bottles
at the stop sign. She doesn't look up,
or maybe she looks up,
but everything right now is a piece of mental magic
so what can they do to her?

I remember when she was young,
the morning I picked her up at the jail and she was leaning
over the counter cursing the clerk and
pulling everything out of the envelope they gave her and throwing it
on the floor screaming until somebody had to come out
and put her back in the cell. That was before she sobered up.
Now she's mild in manner, almost meek, though very opinionated.

She loves these women she writes about,
these rough women raking the bare clay

of some meager Indian domicile who with their hard eyes
and stubbornness are making the best of it.
Everything behind, she writes, *was dead and gone,*
and nothing ahead meant anything.
Grass fires in the distance, the road like a white weathered plank,
and over in the sweathouse, Crazy Horse coming to.

I Try to Remember I Am Dying

I tell myself
about how I won't see Miami
again, or my nephews crunching celery,
I won't talk about Robert Kennedy
or tramp through the marsh
to whales
beached and black on an empty
shore. I pray and
meditate, concentrate on death,
watch certain programs
concerned with failed operations,
point out the way a beauty's face
sags, the stiff
walk of a former lover. I
promote retirement,
attend funerals,
dial my dead mother's number
and harangue the new family
that's got it.
I whisper to a child,
faint with delight,
that I'm a dead man.
He looks at me with contempt,
but I go on talking,
sure I can convince him,
sure I can see, like
a fleck of blood in his eye,
the fatal wound.

Kicking

When we broke up I removed all traces from the house.
The little plastic vials, the inside-out glassine bags
stamped with names: CORVETTE, GRAND PRIX, LEMANS,
dumped the hospital tubing and three blood-stained belts and
the book on medieval farming I used to read
like a lullaby. *I never loved you,*
the furniture said, *I always hated you,*
and all the plants coarsely mocked me.
I waked up with hands clamped to my throat
somewhere applause dying out, the hole getting bigger.
And ground down the space between
us for weeks with women, call them women,
but the minute I was out their door
the hole gaped again, like a pocketbook torn open by a thief. I raged
through the house, explained to the open refrigerator how misused I was,
wept into my hands, puked, sweat the shame
into my sheets, studied my horoscope, scoured texts
in film and print, attended showcases for the chemically deranged,
complied with whatever I was told, got a haircut,
listened to whatever song
said the world was an impossible place, prayed, dreamed—
and was glad, even in the worst dreams,
when I saw the spike—bespoke it
among friends, admitted the stupid maniacal ignorant impossible notions
behind the whole thing,
and was often hurled suddenly a thousand
miles an hour at the desire simply to look at you. Old Horse.
My friend knew a woman getting clean
who stuffed rags into her lover's gas tank
and blew up a block's worth of cars. Another form of undistinguished
pleading, he called it, and laughed. But it's nothing, nothing.
Years ago, just before I left for the war,
a friend and I drove to Jacksonville Beach

and walked out onto the strand
where Hurricane Doreen had whipped the surf
into suds against the breakwater
and the big ocean buoys, as large as tractors, rolled in the waves.
I was bereft then too & men were dying & the wind blew none of it away.

Zen Do

They are teaching us to stay put, as Mother did
in the oh so long ago when her lips tasted of raspberries.
Gradually the trash fires of metaphysics die out.
Behind each of us, we're told, a bank shelves away.
Beyond this a vastness opens.
Yesterday the woods bled all day.
Conversion of thought into a thin gold wedge
is multiple and serial and endless.
Who advances credit for one whose name is not registered,
whose footprints are his only currency?
I sink into the dew to see what my body will leave behind.
At dawn I go out on the lawn
and shadowbox with the green metal Buddha
who does not notice the world crept like a cat into his arms.

Heroin II

No monster in the knife drawer
or the medicine cabinet or the icy woods,
or in a turn for the worse,
   no back stairs kicked loose
by a madman: nothing here but firelight
explaining itself on your face, and dreams we have
of wild animals come into the house
       as if they love us
now, gentled by drugs, who sit with us like merciful children;

and the way you stretch your body like something expensive
& carefully considered,
   about to be put away
for the night, and the way the night continues
despite everything we say about it, a majestic presence
it itself: and the arch of your neck like a natural bridge
joining this farm & heaven—worlds unopposable—the stories
we tell trailing off into murmurs
      & long defenestrating silences
in which great shifts of perspective take place,

and the dog, vacationing next door this week,
and the way we wrote letters
   all one fall
and overcame each one as we wrote it,
and carried them to the mailbox
and hid in the bushes by the road
     waiting for the substitute mailman,
the one who said the dead fields were beautiful, to find them.

Moon, Moon

The moon follows me street by street—
the same moon with its Camembert and blue face,
blue-eyed moon—or a new moon each street,
one per street—whichever it is
I'm faithful to the one I see, singing "Moon River,"
as I go, walking the streets, faithful to the one
I'm with at the moment I'm with her—I'm with
no one now—I take the moon for a symbol of devotion tonight,
of love's grace, moon over the East River,
Hudson delta, over the Atlantic where hurricane's
despoiling an empty patch of sea, warming up—

tonight there's moonlight in the city, pale effusion
upon the shoulders of drummed-out lovers
and torture victims—upon the priest rolling
up a badminton net,
the child teaching herself to pray—
equal opportunity moon, moon of Puerto Rican gangsters
playing dance tunes before work,
moon of the emotionally demolished and crazy—
impeccable moon—vast and uncluttered, moon
of silent blue seas, moon of Asia and its
outlying dependencies—of the Americas & Europe—
chiseled African moon—it's a rock in night's shoe,
light left on in the closet I enter to
root through love's used-up materials
and scrawled utterances—my pleas for reconsideration—
(moon my companion of demented nights
at the pay phone dialing her number . . .)—witness
to the fulgarious *pecca vis* of love—
strabismic moon, you might say, same moon
as in the stories, distant self-contained wilderness
or astral dumping ground—can't-make-it-

on-its-own moon—like me, accepting all compliments,
stubborn, yet quick to take offense, abashed
and fretful moon, moon white with anger—with fright—
incidental moon, you might say—what's left,
I think, thinking of the moon
as I head south across the city, of love
squeezed in a fist—
call it love—white chunk
of gravel in the nightbird's crop—
only one per customer (moon), yet always available,
the two of us not afraid to show our faces, moon,
neither checking out yet on the other, or on life
(this mainly what I'm thinking about—life,
checking out on it, as if down streets
slanting into a mine,
going down, dear, to explore my
mineral wealth—ha ha—
one who's had enough of trickery and
love snatched from his hands—fix that, moon—)
still here, bobbing up—white apple, head
of a newborn baby, moon shaped like a city—
shining on millionaires recently stripped of their holdings,
on the last customer in Show World, picking the dried
moon fizz from his fingers—egg, imponderable,
bull's-eye—I'm faithful to you tonight, moon,
one more undependable lover
talking a stroll, pretending to walk it off,
headed into the rural districts,
of Central Park, that is, toward the little
homesteads brightened by longing
and flashlights—cracked, moony hearts
sputtering like engines about to fail—

you'll find me stretched out on the grass, dear,
singing "Moon Over Charlie,"

supine under my one moon, which is mine & everyone's,
like life, or love—crazed again—
once more—stupefied as a matter of fact,
without negotiable resources or plans,
discommoded and jittery—how I run on—
moon like a fumbled button, doorknob
on a portal I throw myself against—or did—
who would believe me—she wouldn't—
one more time.

Dreams

I wake early from a dream of French poetry,
from the wellsprings of it, all rural in the dream:
a cripple in blue britches limps to a mossy well
contradicting himself as he comes.

Morning is a continuation of the dream
—the rusty, crippled hours, trees as if dipped in light syrup,
skaters coasting by, one man in black, drifting with arms folded . . .

I read over a few poems, make some changes in my mind,
dilute fabrications, push across a desert colored red
by sunset, bridge a gap in
the last scene between lovers
now too frail and bored to go on.

My mother was in my dream,
commenting on my looks and the way I dress.
You're too formal, she says.

     the early morning hours
extend generously into day

I read Italian poets; leftwing, outraged poets
from the Sixties (poets who are always leaving home),
and Pasolini,
distorted and enraged by lust,
a concentrate,
a man in a silver sidecar, the late poems
unburdening themselves of poetry

. . . and read a story
about a woman dreaming, who opens
fruit after fruit, orange pulp

and red squashed material
she doesn't understand, who watches her son
place speckled cowries on her sleeping body, a backward boy . . .

each dream without relation to the day
catching its breath up ahead,

day a novelty
appearing at the exits of sleep,
a concession stand employee
who is actually your father.

My father once
in a cowboy suit outside school
performing poorly executed rope tricks.

The Submerged Fields

It's late and someone's almost forgotten
how to write, how to
turn the jubilated rough fields into fields where
the moon scatters pleasantries, fields the wind picks at
looking for bones, fields his ancestors rode over,
died in, where his father's buried
and the misshapen crepe myrtle
sags in sunlight, sags in rain . . .

someone sent out a cover story for his life,
but you know that, you can tell . . .

it's late and someone's almost forgotten
how to convince you he's telling the truth,
how the breeze stirs memories in him,
how the river's an adept of paradise
and each cone and disinterred patch of light
each meadowlark and vole are precious
to someone . . . someone no one talks to anymore
is on the road, it's late
and he's almost forgotten how to speak,
how to convince himself there's enough to go on,
how the fields, rained-on and the crops drowned,
might be married to something else
besides failure, someone who stops
to observe how the light pours through the rain
and the road's washed through to the clay
underlayment which is white and shines,

who gets up late and writes

How beautiful the days are here
and the river matted with ferns touches my heart.

Visitation

Fall binds itself, sticks itself loosely in tufts
      and fragments into trees, goes bad in an oak,
drains color down the long sleeve of a catalpa
      like a cut getting worse.
The woman who washes at the water fountain is gone now,
      drifting among the avenues;
her place in the plan is kept for her by certain
      small arrangements made years ago and honored in
relays: same bottles, different men. Now the cross-hatched,
      sugary light smells of the open doors of Chinese restaurants;
a breeze sweeps into the slim upper branches of a maple,
      stirs the leaves to a frenzy, fades, and reappears
twirling on the sidewalk; for a second
      there's no pattern to things, no scheme.
The aged couple feeding pigeons by hand, a vicious pair,
      pause; the old man stares straight ahead,
the woman too, adjusting her clothes;
      whatever they see—a moment ago wasn't there.

Washington Square

Fellow passes my bench, wheels his bike
around, screams, leaps off and throws himself lengthwise
onto grass, stares straight into the sun. Odor of alcohol,
this about the only thing these days
produces such floppy flamboyance,
the idea's to give life meaning, drama, I am somebody
kind of buffing, but it always fails. I read Mallarmé,
don't pay attention, try some Baraka,
"The New World" one of the best poems in the new world,
wonder again about B's use of parentheses, what's up
with that, let my attention rise into the sycamores,
dusty crumpled leaves the color of shredded cigarettes,
sunlight on the bum again, time when
our good fortune to be alive is treacly with sadness,
but good, affordable feeling, a statutory melancholy,
fine to feel set against the true horrors of our time,
faintly celebratory, sought after by poets
and others of the feeling professions, it gets to you,
but no noticeable difference in passersby, they push
on, it's warm today, day if there was a pond around
there'd be gold dust on the surface, leaves floating
gently nipped by trout. I think of Emily Dickinson's
great poems about the seasons, and lately, so I recall,
I've been thinking of Sir Philip Sidney, of Wyatt
and of the Earl of Surrey who wrote Wyatt's elegy, a formal
and regular practice in those days—Mallarmé continued this—
poets setting themselves at the head of the grave
to bless and keep a foot on the fallen great.
In the anthology not many major practitioners these days,
lonely profession even if a feature of courtly life,
the great always lonely as Socrates taught us, all
of us lonely as the rest of us taught us . . . a friend
I called was weeping, couldn't stop, loneliness again,

if it goes on too long unchecked we make bitter mistakes
or sometimes knock on the neighbor's door and new life begins,
that is, love starts, finds a way
to notice the light in the oaks, soft flight
of words or birds winging over us, the beauty
of mercy, the drunk's delicate fingers,
a figure that connects and exemplifies us. A poem
does this, or the truth admitted. For better or worse,
we admit only universal truths, but there are as many
of the individual variety perhaps, not grave but lasting,
we find these out by living. A breeze snakes along the grass.
It seems to follow sunlight, sunk there.
Now the whole park's in shadow. Sun's still strong
against the upper parts of the eastern buildings, shines
all the way through the top floors of one, exposing
desks, a Brazilian flag, two women gesturing furiously.
Snappy, birdlike, fluttery light; then night suddenly comes.

Bontemps

Figure you could spend a thousand years
studying one speck of butterfly dust, then go on
to the next and then ten thousand on the water drop the speck
floats in, the ground-up regurgitated
mucilage its accompanying amoeba has just ejected from its excretal sac
taking up another three thousand years of patient
intent scrutiny, and then the germ in the amoeba's innards
another five hundred years, and the refraction of light passing through this,
the fourth wave or conniption of particles from
the right set of rainbowlike protuberances, take this
as your area of expertise, spend ten millenniums
tracing it back to the source which of course is a sumptuous
spangolem in itself and includes the spurt of burning gases just now passing
Jupiter's third moon, one faint wisp of this containing
enough hydrogen to power earth for a million years,
take a grain of this and stand by yourself on Copernicus,
in a dusty hole, scrutinize the periodicity of the four hundredth
atom to the left of the Seal of St. John, and wait
your turn with the five billion others who have
themselves spent eternity doing exactly the same
thing, at a slightly different pace,
to explain this, and while you are waiting
under the one trillion billion stars upon which
the molecules—worlds aspin—all quake, each with its own separate
and sonorous rhythm, each awaiting its turn at the mike,
each impatient, put upon, outraged, desperate
like a man in a dark stairwell fighting off thieves,
and while you are waiting think how one
moment of time is enough in which to understand everything,
one glance at a single tree holding up the rain-shattered light, enough,
and then turn back and start over because you remember a miscalculation
somewhere in the third era to the left of the beginning,
and do this several times, all the time maintaining

your place in line, and then you realize it's been going on like this
for years, like somebody's idea of the good life,
or the way each night the cooks and the busboys gather
on DeLawter's back steps and smoke and tell stories
passing a bottle around, eating crab legs, and summer never ends.

Santa Monica

Someone was writing this incredibly personal poem
and I was reading it over his shoulder
Santa Monica was in the poem
but you could hardly tell
and the devastating loss of integrity
his wife ranting
his cowardice—these were in the poem
and he was sweating as he wrote it
and looking around as if for spies
I am amazed he didn't see me
but sometimes they look right through you
he went on writing his act of contrition
and memory
expressing his extreme embarrassment and sorrow
at how he selfishly used loved ones
lost the money and the house
sat in the car out in the driveway the last morning
and couldn't think where to go
until someone, a cop maybe, suggested
he get something to eat, and then after that he drove
to Kansas. There was a weeping blue cypress in the poem
and at one point he was very accurate about how it feels
when on the street the beloved turns you away.
Sometimes, he wrote, I stand unnoticed at a counter, waiting.
At last the woman looks at me and asks what.
It was a struggle, for both of us, to get to the next part.

The Waters of the Deep

We were trying to keep it conversational,
close to the text,
but I was very nervous that year, all year,
and kept breaking in to express an inexpressible sorrow,
and when we turned around—we
were in the garden—I saw his wife pouring some red liquid into a pot,
red like neon . . . or no,
red like the heroin/blood mix
swirling like the waters of the deep
in a syringe,
and I thought how the narrative, the story
simply branches off in unrecoverable directions,
things mount up, experiences,
the way she said *sulty* for *salty*,
distinguished moments I mean anguished moments,
until sometimes I think I am back in prison,
some medium-security place
where I'd look through the fence at cars
turning in to the strip mall,
and as ugly as the mall was with its stores the color of pigeon feathers
and the dust on the cars,
the boarded-up seafood restaurant & the crystal shop,
I'd wish I could go there,
at least use the pay phone in private, call my past up,
maybe my old camp counselor,
tell him I'd be late for dining hall,
but I was on my way.

You can see how it would be possible
simply to go on like this, constructing little scenarios,
foolish responses to life,
to stimuli,
to love and its evasions,

go on tormenting myself
with the vastness of losing propositions,
to say, Well, I'm not sure,
but I think this came after that,
or was it at the same time,
waiting, as if at a bus stop in Puebla,
for someone simply
to describe something in English,
pull a pig's knuckle
from his pocket and pass this around
while he talks in a low voice of a woman
who used to beat him with switches,
something like this,
some way of putting things that captures
something otherwise unendurable,
some last chance exemplified, rain pitting the ditch water
while she sang softly to herself a song
I no longer remember, her voice fading into the rain
and into her life's slow insistence on leaving me.

"It's almost like this," he said, my friend,
lowering his voice,
"yet only collaterally, since what you are saying
occurred in *your* life, not mine,
but I do think this is what happens generally,
something profound occurs one afternoon in the kitchen
or in the alley where your uncle
broke down and wept,
and later you stand around talking,
hesitating to explain,
to say why, that year you complied
with everything, you kept losing the car keys,
and called your ex-mother-in-law repeatedly
until she took out an order of protection
against you, and then—

what was it?—you had to give up the drugs,
and later—tonight maybe—
after too many cups of coffee,
we stand out back watching a train rattle by,
and when the guy next to you asks
what you are thinking, you say,
'I was thinking of throwing myself under the wheels,'
but that's not it. Right? That's not even close."

East End

Framed hard against daylight, against day, plush gray sky slanted west,
we rise, fall down the dune and run at the sea. It's almost calm, snaky under silk,
an army transferring matériel under cover, approaching us. Light picks up
the failed sheen of soaked sand draining. Rock sand, rocks, scoria rubbed
to egg shapes, mottled or striped, some gray, formal, black-suited
dolmen to place on top of a wall you walk by to a funeral—sea rocks.
Up ahead, ponderous clay cliffs, ocher cliffs, broken off, chewed at,
crumbling, stare out to sea. Arches undercut verticals. Each element's
in for the long haul, nothing going anywhere, it's clear; everything repeats itself,
picks up what passes by & uses this, keeps at it. Torn skate purses, crumbled lace of bone,
crab claws, crab shells like tiny tricorns: something awful's happened
under the sea. The dunes rear back, appalled, tumble down and bury themselves
under grass. Something's buried there, that's what it looks like: summer and its dead,
the age sinking deeper. We're following the slink of tideline, watching it run optimistically up
and recede. It goes on rustling, rolling up, the paunchy surf bullying it behind,
orbiculate, unable to repeat itself exactly, unable to conclude, which is the lure.
Sure. One minute to the next nothing's the same, inconclusive, only the invariable
materials, procedure, repetition, the loading docks in continuous operation,
big payloaders, stinking of the Mesozoic, chuffing up, crunching against the ramps,
the enterprise going under lamplight, firelight and sunny day,
combining or sorting out, slipping one thing inside the frame of another,
using what it has, making do, the same ingredients, same elements
always in short supply, the effort hampered by bad weather
and the torpor agitation replaces, by inexactitude and irrepressible revision,
someone dying on his feet, the light beginning to fail, everything
piled against the same limitation, the transaction now surely giving way
like an ocean turning ponderously on its heel, catching itself in the face
with a blow—a wave, salt-streaked, white-streaked—collapsing and rising again.

At This Hour

The city deharmonizes in some areas, arms us with breastworks,
yet continues to provide juxtapositions both instructive and beautiful,
a constabulary in the mind,
archways through which light tosses lightly its yellow exigencies,
in others
a sense of the casual ribaldry of existence,
or diverts us down increasingly narrow passageways
until we find ourselves once more leaning out over darkness itself,
unable to confide in our dearest friends, disestablished and bereft,
commonplace characters who have become withdrawn.

The city does this
or the willingness to go . . . to get on with things
does. Without waiting for amplitude to swell in the lower keys
we maintain swampy
and undistinguished unions with desperate characters
to sustain this. It's always best to
hope for the next generation's success, but not so easy.
We don't really care, subdue what we can now, devalue the rest.

A fortune, someone says commenting on this,
would complete things nicely, though today, as the wind picks up,
I am thinking of summer's references, the Rubens exhibit
we got sick in, and then a brief shower of rain,
the city's version of beneficence, falls prostrate
among the tuned-up and sparkling late afternoon sunlight,
and the vertigo begins to pass, which is the key, things move along,
the humiliating set of circumstances reverts to type,
and our carefully pleaded argument, love's lost soldier, fades
along the surface rhythms of some obscure chant
playing softly on a junkie's turned-down radio, someone almost peaceful at this hour.

from WOMEN OF AMERICA

Eastern Forests

I have been walking in the eastern forests
through everglades and hammocks into a mixed deciduous woodland
where hummingbirds and woodpeckers cohabit in the downy hawthorn bushes
and the pepper-and-salt skipper moth, hunted
by the white-eyed vireo and other creatures,
batters its way through broken branches of shortleaf pine
and smooth sumac, a senseless bug without what we call heart,
though as everyone knows some intention, impervious to special pleading,
propels this creature and the eastern black oak acorn weevil,
among thousands of others, across vast reaches of transition, mixed
deciduous and oak-hickory forests, along with wood frogs and flying squirrels,
like love does in our nomenclature, or rumors of gold.

There's Trouble Everywhere

There the blind man and his personal dark,
dawn like an emission between buildings,
arrested in the street a second,
meline, no, saffron, a peckish, dilute yellow
and uncontrollable like the light in
a Lorrain painting,
the dawn bearing down out
of its momentary stall,
there the blind man avec dog,
a man who can't suddenly dash
across the street crying *Martha, is it you?*
but must wait
for the dog's slow mind to consider
the next step. And those black wings leaving the scene,
the creases of analgetic green in the young trees
like the heaviness in the shoulders
after adolescence, the
description of life's deeper meaning
in the curve of the homeless man's body, asleep
on his sweater, the young woman walking fast
who looks as if small bits of veneer
have been chipped away, these
speak of something important just arriving.
An old obsession's slowly dying. The day
refers to itself in the third person, like the grinning maniac
who greets you as if he knows you. It's always
morning somewhere, you think,
but this doesn't have any hold on you now.
Even as you move you are reaching back
for something, some lien on existence
you remember, some slab or kitchen step you sat on
listening to the interior noises, the rhythm—you
say to yourself now—of a continuity

you haven't been able to find since,
but it isn't that easy, and it never was.
Always some criminal loose on the property,
moving closer. Some name you
once went by
inscribed inside the wedding band
of an unidentified corpse pulled from the river.
And the love you were so sure of,
that appears like a shape in the trees
on a leeward reach, the vast greenery
uprooted from some rain forest empire,
squeaks and trembles, or this
is only the blur cornering on Tenth.
Whatever might change what's wrong
won't declare itself. And the young poet,
an austere woman briskly climbing
the stairs at the Cineplex, looks
haggard and close to despair,
but says nothing as you pass; it's not necessary
at this time to beg rescue, not yet,
though summer's heavy on the town,
and the well-watered lawn
by the cathedral's not open to our citizens.

What This Stands For

Plum bushes unable to bear
       the light and the pond that has no place to hide
the reeds saying save me save me are lying

as are the deer imitating lawn ornaments
       and the cherry trees with their little pink
collapsible mouths. The greasy surf,

triplicated and distressed,
       mixed in design, performs
its one trick, lying about it, too,

promoting its complexity,
       which is nothing of the sort. The stupid desire
to find something else with an interior light, some bug

or monkey,
       some planet or lover turning away,
the sexual context of memory

is almost too much
       in this beachy spring with its wet towels
and donuts

gritty with aspirin dust,
       the rabbits like small brown hats
littering the yard.

Here comes that feeling again,
       the emotional ineptitude that abruptly picks up its bed
and walks, that you come on later standing drinks

and roaring, the one that knows
       how to deal with difficult women
and the dark innuendo everyone calls a love life.

Women of America

On the pale morning I left town
I was thinking about women,
and later, in the Rockies where work was scarce,
I thought of women all day
and pretended I was in Florida, for example,
at the little business opportunity my friend Calico
ran in the mall at Perry. By roads in the desert
and among the bean fields in California
I thought of women and
preserved this huge interior life for them
like an estate sheltered from creditors.
It was better, like Dante, to have the woman
out of sight, to spend my time thinking about her,
like Petrarch, like the crippled Leopardi, Keats
and all the rest, to save myself the trouble of real life
and the provincialisms of fact, all that,
the women somewhere maybe in heaven
or upstate New York, doing something
besides thinking of me, I didn't mind,
the conversation went on anyway, its riches sustained me,
the complex multifactors crossing
and intermixing like a high school band
in its difficult formations. Everything else
was simple gesturing, an arm reaching out a car window
to hand someone a sandwich. Of what this came to,
I can't really speak, the women
in their trials and compacts, their anguished disputes
outside small-town jails, of these
I have nothing to say. I was seized by thought,
on a pale morning in Alabama,
distracted as I pumped gasoline, wondering
about Hazel and the grip
she still had on me—How so, Hazel, I thought,
and thus time began to pass, in America.

Monkeys in White Satin

Now and then you catch a glimpse of space invaders
moving around under the bridge—campers, someone says.
Once—this may be a dream—the road by my house
was lined with blossoming plums. White like
the foamy sweat of torture victims,
residue of tessellated stars, something less particular
than we would have liked. Convinced of my importance
I moved to another town. No one even noticed
how benumbed I was. You could get a monkey
back then for a pet. Always, without exception,
you'd regret it if you did. Later we were at the beach,
old friends, or calling ourselves such,
the tide a dark hesitating force that came on anyway,
like some reference you made to what's next in line
that you said meant nothing, wasn't your intention at all.

Recall

Old cadences, cracklings along the sight line,
your arms thrown back, I remember this,

the tortured way with your second language,
what was instrumental, the spiritual phrasing,

cups of tea, an afternoon in Venice
overcoming resistance, who could forget,

you said: *The garden like a strangled lover*
lies heaped upon itself,

and no one laughed, the stillness of the afternoon,
electrical cicadas, the sun offering

to pay for everything, the world filled
to the brim, you noticed this, later the star

jasmine vines stripped naked,
hurricane disorderly and evil-tempered,

like us, you said, everything just then—painted plates,
the operatics—referring to this.

In July

In July when meat smoke
fills the town,
that's when I think
of you. And June, too,
I thought of you in June.
And in the months before that.
A string of time's divisions, all
of them inky
with little dots where I
thought of you.
Certain places soaked
with you, like the towels they used to
mop up the lemonade.
I thought of you
in the band concert
when the tubas
sank down into their difficult valley.
And later at the reception
where a boy dropped a slice of yellow cake
into the punch.
In July the barbecues begin.
As if it's then the cows reach the market,
meat available.
In China, they say,
men fish with nets in the little streams.
Landlords watch them, waiting
for their money.
If I was there,
an intense person, watching his net
settle onto the current,
I'd think of you, that's obvious.

Shame

I keep referring to you in transition from
one state of being to another like a woman you see
on two or three different buses in the same afternoon.
But this is not shame exactly or anything numinous
and I can't tell you how badly
I want to get high and walk under big complicated trees
and keep talking about you
until you show up. Love goes like this: You forget.
I'm trying not to let this happen, it's a kind of workout
I'm giving myself, high impact, me pounding against
your silence. They all know where you are.
And foolishly I haunt the stockyards and the record stores.

Compared to What

The way certain rogues get to us,
the way, coming into a town,
the tottery chimneys, the creamery,
the boy stumbling as if he understands what it is to be broken,
the way these move us slightly.

. . .

And how on another day
someone takes a room in a hotel and calls a few friends,
and orders a prostitute,
and tells her a story
of paddling a boat among drifting flower gardens,
and the woman, who is not interested, who is thinking of soup
or an envelope waiting at home,
shifts toward the man
lightly touching him, grazing his arm,
without feeling anything for him,
simply doing what she is paid to do, and the man,
who knows this, and doesn't care especially,
is thinking of the flowers drifting in the river, gardenias and roses,
and of a gar, silvery and sharp like a sword, cutting just under the surface.

The way when we hear this we sink down
as if we are entering a small enclosure in our minds
and are suddenly overcome with despair.

And there is another story one remembers
in which a young person
comes into money and becomes prideful

and loses everything and takes a job in a sale barn
wearing a straw hat and making jokes that aren't funny,
and as we listen, a sudden, irrepressible tenderness enters us.

Later there will be stories told in basement rooms,
cold sandwiches on a counter
and a faint chilled laughter from the porch,
and someone who hasn't spoken for a week gets up
and pisses noisily in a can . . .

I was thinking of a woman I loved,
who wouldn't love me.
I thought I would never get past this,
and though it was obvious I would,
that we all do, I began to love the pain
that didn't want to go away, and held on to it.

It touches me how ignorant we are
of many simple effects, the way after my
father stamped through the garden his shoes smelled of flowers.
The way as he badgered us we could smell the wet dirt
and the rotted lilies.

And how later we put our experiences to ourselves
with a certain fastidious pride,
and compel ourselves,
as if we are friends of the court,
to address certain facts that would go otherwise unnoticed,
and how there is a way of explaining these conflictions
to a friend
that makes them seem unimportant.

And the way someone we pass in the street,
an old woman out early
who is too heavy and aches with gout
and favors one grandchild over another and
is slightly desperate and afraid for money—the way
we pass her without caring who she is, and how this
is what it is to be human, no one very close
after all, and how obvious it is—like spring
taking over everything—what we want.

• • •

Soon it is night again and we are wandering around
outside the house thinking things over,
weighing the dark
like a puppy in our hands,
dividing our life into phases,
trying to place one bit of sadness on top of another,
attempting, so we believe, to experience the whole of ourselves,
which has doubled back,
trying to establish representation
with what is already gone,
sure now there was
nothing we could do to save ourselves
and trying not to be scared by this, comparing ourselves
to someone gentled by loss, to a young teacher perhaps,
standing in a darkening classroom
the day of the hurricane, lingering after the children have gone
watching the sky darken and the wind begin to pick at the trees,
a woman who knows something irreplaceable
is dying in her . . .

• • •

understanding how it is possible to place our whole life
succinctly into a frame such as this,
again and again, yet never able
to turn away and leave it there . . .

trying to make something
up that is strong enough to hold us
or move us or keep us.
Like a man in a field walking in the wind
who briefly forgets himself in the smell of lemongrass,
who comes on a red scurry of fur and bone
and stops, convinced an age of unhappiness has arrived.

• • •

Won't you at least, she says, consider
another way of putting things—

and later,
after a good meal, the way we explain we were off our stride,
that is to say impossible to live with . . .

and in the dream, her fiancé's laughter
humiliated us,
the way she wouldn't say where they were going on the honeymoon . . .
for a moment this wasn't a dream . . .

• • •

In Miami the stacked blue waves tumble in.

You can look up a description of the place
in a book in the lobby and and then glance up
and see the "coconut palms
and sparkling pool, the Kontiki bar
and wide white sand beach . . ."

Whatever looks straight, she said,
it might look straight, but it eventually curves.
And I said
is that supposed to mean something?
But by then it was too late to come to an understanding.

• • •

The way occasionally we greet the dawn as if we are responsible for it.

Modern Art

Matisse, in a letter
to Henry Clifford, said an artist must identify himself
with the rhythms of nature, make effort,
prepare the soil, get down and grub. Where you end up
won't look like the place you started in.
It won't be that place. I'm obsessed with a woman
and each day I invite the shadow shape—
which obsession is—in the door. Lingerer,
vague disamplitude, you're like rain
in the next county. I sense your presence on the breeze,
smell your body in the damp clay and feculence.

Late Days

1. OUTSIDE LAS VEGAS

In the Silver Dollar john
I place my hand flat on the sink
wrench around
& look at my face to see what happened.
Later I watch someone's neighbor undress
then hit herself across the back with a cat-o'-nine-tails
before lights out. I walk around incognito
in my own home. Dispatcher
of long-distance affections,
the twenty-eighth caller on the call-in show,
the one who gets abruptly nasty & begins to weep,
I signal for a time-out.
My best friend became a doctor at forty,
sits alone
in his office eating sardine sandwiches
practicing his technique.
It's the heart, he says, it's
diabetes, prostate, that'll be two hundred dollars.
We used to strip
down & examine each other's equipment.
Persuaded by the heart of things,
by time spent there alone,
we believed in life, in the life to come.
Now I'm traveling to Mexico by stake truck,
riding in the back. Dressed by a fire,
among friends,
I compare dog bites & episodes w/ the Virgin,
and make big claims about my capacity for love.
In the right-
hand pocket of my former life I've left something for you.
That is, darling, your turn will come.

I'd walk out on myself if I could.
I love the distant glow in the nighttime desert sky
like a worn yellow spot in the dark
everything might still slip through.

Pursued by Love's Demons

As if the backstreets of our local city
might dispense with their Pyrrhic accumulation of dust and wineful tonality,
offer a reprise of love itself, a careless love
rendered grand and persuasive
by its own shy handful of hope, some ballast such as this
on a summer afternoon when the air smells of slaughtered chickens,
and other problems, like the estranged spouse of a good friend,
holler from the passageway. It's always conclusive
in the bungled moment after you try to accomplish something irreducible.
So you say as you return empty-handed from the store,
having forgotten everything—your money, the list.

Solitude

In the background a disturbance builds:
camarones; bone spurs;
individualism adding up to what?
You beat about
finding space for all your goods.
I know how it is.
Chunky, ill-defined,
life lumbers on. You wish you could remember
that German word—
      a kind of sugar cake;
the solitude she entered
like a phrase dispelling doubt,
the solitude
entrained and crowded now
something—something—weeded out.

Old Business

for L.W.

A quiet joy appears amid loneliness, doesn't
replace it. We pass the South American men
listening to a radio played softly.
We put faith—in love, old songs, grace
like a gold ring
left by the sink—in what abides;
we put faith in what returns, forget
easily. I read a poem;
it's one the poet wrote just before he died.
There's death in the poem, though I don't believe
he anticipated his own. I think he looked up
from the desk a little shaken
and soothed. But even this, someone says,
is no formula, or even an illustration.
The wish to perceive is itself a mistake, limited,
not one of the aspects. Yet we catch sight
of a pattern disappearing in the mix,
waves from a distance
like comb tracks, claw marks,
the young girl in the foreground
lifting her hands into her dark hair.
An amplitude that closes on itself appeals,
a certain wild hillside ransacked by light.

Talking to Whom

I am like a man
swallowing small fish whole.
Afterward he watches TV,
coughing quietly into his fist.
If I rub my naked belly around
on the floor, where will you be,
in which room, talking on the phone?
It's at moments like these some tragic
element, some quip
or piece of hotel furniture
flies out the window. Little reaper,
Jefe, there was something else
I wanted to say. I've investigated
all this. And stood among the market's
bright fruit weeping openly.
Dearest, they are tearing
down the movie theaters—
blackened areas in which
we clutched each other,
leaving marks.

Each Night I Enter a Terrible Silence

We demonstrated procedures
for each other, taking turns
playing the extraterrestrial. I managed
to corner some affection one night
and gave it to you, a small chunk
you fried up for supper. It took
several glasses to wash it down.
We never could say much
about the future, but insisted on trying.
We thought a lot, but kept it to ourselves.
You were the one passing in the hall
that dark night, a shape like a burglar
I spoke to softly so as not to disturb my wife.

Call Girls

My rage, you bet,
and its spectacular aftermath, the visits from the cops,
the cut-rate pharmacies where
I bought medicine,
the all-night theaters
I retired to,
let me justify this,
the downtowns deserted by all but their most
persistent citizens,
the cries from two streets
over
as the pack began to circle back,
all this, I promise you,
explicable,
the covenants unalluded to,
the supermarkets I got stranded in,
the old girlfriends I called and out of consideration
for their new circumstances
never identified myself to,
all these,
a matter of reason, of consequence—
the particular block on Sunset
near some palm trees
where I faltered,
unable to go on,
the Mexican couple I mistook for informers,
the spectacular sunsets in that
part of the world,
the slow aging of affection,
the disputes, the roaring in traffic,
the conversion I reneged on,
something—maybe
you remember—to do with pride

and a diffident manner, some idea—
as I said—I was once
devoted to.

The Night Won't Stop It

We are tired of arguing about who is the most hurt.
Better to toddle off for a little Chinese.
The locust flowers each year like cornmeal in the gutters.
An extraordinary way of putting things, saved up
for the love affair of the century,
gets used by a baker's apprentice talking to his dog.
Investors sink back into the shadows.
Someone with a huge capacity for ambivalence nods off.
The cut-rate sky seems for a moment to throb.
Affairs that began in spring's alarming weather die of heatstroke.
A generous gesture hovers in the back of the mind,
but never steps forward. Cravings appear,
like baskets of fresh linen, in the homes of our friends.
Tenderness is appraised and turned in for theft.
The fragrance of dispatched gardens, like a telegram
from the government, is just a memory. It is so fitful,
so desperate, this business of what matters.
Another's down with a stroke. This way of looking at things
will be forgotten. It was only an experiment.

Creation Rites

. . . some average of the holiness in every person you have run into,
consider this, something like a wall covered in green vines,
an emblem for the spirit, or if not that, what happens when two lovers
stand among bushes in a garden off Houston, arguing a little, but afraid
really to get into it because they fear winding up alone,
and then several music lovers or ex-drug takers wandering along
on a summer day past the restaurant supply stores and the vacant
lot where the wino hotel used to be, they're walking to Chinatown,
these holy people like pilgrims in Benares where they are talking
about putting crocodiles into the river to eat the corpses, you probably heard about it,
and there is some question about procedure in the cremation rites, all that,
but they're obviously part of it, too, the holiness, and still it's summer
and my friend has changed into her bathing suit and is walking
the three blocks to the public pool, it's getting kind of late, she'll swim
twenty laps and finish as the lifeguard, a slender boy with an island accent,
waits for her to come up out of the water like a rectified god.

A Selection Process

. . . under unrivaled fresh weather, each day random variations,
assurances come, studious, revised sensibility occupies itself.
I walk around, notice the impeccable configurations,
distortions the breeze replaces itself with
in the large philodendron-like trees, massive
spills of wind, a sort of alternating current
of air streaming above my head. When I am walking
tortured by my troublesome life sometimes
I stop in the middle of an ocean of wind
and begin to make swimming motions or I watch
the patterns the dying sun makes with the big oleanders the
shadows placed artfully against the high school
even doves balanced on an electrical wire can be seen
silhouetted in this arrangement. An old woman carrying groceries
passes on my right, moves her lips slightly but doesn't speak.
Soon, before anyone notices, all this will be gone.
So many claim they lie awake wishing for a new
design, better implants. Yesterday a woman in wind-whipped clothes
led her child on bikes around the corner, admonishing her
to keep pedaling, but the child sped along
I could see in her eyes
her power, the child's power; a distant
line of palms, like fiends in the mind, began to wave.
How close we come, I think, to a life very different from this one.

Excursion

The heart moves on, selects a place for itself,
tossed down destitute it rises, only the mind
gives up, a winter's tale
dispersed into scenery around a muddle of ideas,
someone edges out of the park
to say something about irrefutable joy, lost
among the swarming cabs, it rains all afternoon,
streaks on windows, the bays, indented spaces before buildings,
gutters, scuffed patches in Central Park, all fill up,
later we find the subway's a gray lake, a solitary cat swimming,
desolation's investments repay handsomely,
somehow we are not surprised or sidetracked.

Religious Art

Certain precautions, obstacles
set against vandals—the stretch
of highway, for example, outside Nichols, New Mexico,
loneliness like a family art,
a man's idea of himself
pinned down in the Holy Land, strings of peppers
drying on a porch.

I press hard with my feet
against the earth and
call this fighting back. All yesterday
I walked around counting birds.
Trees, a spray of pebbles in the forecourt,
a dip the wind took about six

maintain the posts assigned, repel boarders.

The peculiar emptiness
in the mown hayfield this afternoon
we stood staring into—as a precaution—
the clefts and shadowy declines containing
our deepest interests, the grass shining and then going dull against
the fading light, these were protection enough.

Arrangements

I'd like to try a maneuver that doesn't "start in silence
    and end in frenzy," but instead begins
in a terrific caterwauling, thrashing and flailing,
    the fists banging against the floor, cries and
shrieks, appalling in its verisimilitude,
    crashing, writhing delirium, berserk ruction
and development extended into distraught maniacal pleading,
    convulsion, feverish excited speech, hysterical
slapping scenes, a nucleonic furor, and goes
    on from this into an unexpected hallucinatory
passage in which I extoll the beauties of mountain lakes
    at dawn, the strained—while I do this—
look on my face held for hours while I explain
    how beasts and deranged parental figures
did this to me, tried to drown me, all the while
    patting some obviously organic material
I've collected in a sack. You know what
    I'm talking about. Horror at the heart
of beauty. And so I continue, into the whimpering
    and begging stage, the puerile confession episode
in which I convict myself of all manner of hate crimes
    and offer myself up for special punishment.
Then the little chat with the warden.

    A quiet time. Then the priest where I smile sweetly
and enter a beatific state. There's something in my eye.

    I never know who they mean. And despite everything,
silence comes.

Sprung

The ministerial shapes of
Chinese women
in the garden I mean, red

fetishistic flowers,
the ropy
sun-damaged hollyhocks

all that's left to put
momentarily against
the crimes of our nature,

the vertigo,
come forth
now, this young boy

among the earnestness
the coziness of commerce,
to carry a hose

and untidily water
everything,
wearing silver bracelets, alone

with his task
as we all are,
the time when dear Kiser

was alive, my parents, too,
and Oscar, and
Kate,

the boy
missing all those spots,
like I did.

Dusk at Homer's

The sun withdraws into its twilight years,
into forgetfulness & dreams.
Hard to forget what once we had,
but I'd rather,

rather move on. Ducks in the city,
wildlife in the city, birds:
a list of sightings
tacked to the St. Luke's garden shed: vireos,

a brown thrasher, tanager, shrike.
Who saw those birds?
Some historian, I guess,
Someone with time to kill.

Or now we just say things.
I say she loves me & that's what it is,
say Pesco's still alive,
still talking Aquinas as he cooks.

And that fall when a storm
blew all the leaves out of the trees
and the football field on Saturday was ankle deep
in yellow & red tatters,

we scampered in our satin suits
through them.
An old man in the window is reading a book out loud,
maybe, like me,

skipping the bad parts.
A woman nearby's
got a squared-off look. She took
the average of herself and went with that.

I try to remember what
we used to say about things,
how we put it to ourselves.
I don't know, do you?

I've got time on my hands,
it won't wash off.

Day 7 / 24

Each day arrives in pieces, it's easy to put together, every-
one does it, the functions appear, those paid to revolve rapidly begin,
others gape, some welcome despair, a righteousness flaps like tattered flags,
no one believes this crap, each would like to speak truly, live
with no cause for regret,
I take off my fake silver wings and
stare out at the lawn where nothing much is happening, only night
collecting and disposing of itself, the vegetable kingdom, distant uneasy dogs.

The Moment Preceding

A reverie, small fabrication
of silence, some amulet or woven purse,
some moment in which the languor
is preceded by quiet, this moment comes
first in the dawnlight,
a deep and peculiar clarity, peered into,
some color scheme barely perceptible, this
silence
in which the rigorously fought-out nightwar, the peace
established through centuries of tedious
negotiation, is not blown away
or thrown aside but breached nonetheless
by a simple, barely detectable epistemology,
this tiny shift in consciousness itself,
expressed just now by the scent of gardenias.

Old Nobodies Traveling Alone

Like the hand of God

sweeping backward along a passing train,
like a hand
moving down hip-length hair,

say coppery hair, summer in Antwerp,

lindens in bloom
and the architectural students
giving up righteousness for drugs,

around then
when reports burned
under shady circumstances,

then—like the hand of God we said—

all these elements, corsages
floating in the bowl
you dunked your face in,

love all razory
and dulce—the time before

you conformed
to the unfathomable circumstances
of your next position—

just then, the robin said,
before I could really sing,

we were speaking of turncoats,
tableaux,
the formal arrangement

in which the circumstantial lover

alternated with his own dismay,
the two of them—we're part of this—
contingent, fretful, moving steadily

across the space that was left.

The Wilderness

I think of cities that have vanished into time.
I'm sister to the rain. The trees plunge like dolphins
and the city's a ship diving in the sea.
Everything vanished just a moment ago.
I recall my shame at having to watch my father
be humiliated. They made him recant everything he'd said.
And then praise them. My father the poet, who was never strong.

Even in a city, my friend says,
all you have to do is look up to see wilderness. He means the sky,
weather and such. Once he lived in a hogan out in Arizona.
And got caught sexually pestering an Indian schoolgirl and
went to jail for it. Then he moved to New York
and became a fabric designer. He has a shop over on Madison.

Carthage. Nineveh. Chandrapore.
Mostly the important cities didn't disappear.

"We took a boat up the Ganges, but we had to get out;
all the floating corpses made my wife sick. You can
get too much of that in a hurry. We caught a train
and that was much better, though even in the first-class car
we couldn't avoid the smells. India is in the smells,
don't let anyone tell you different."

AND MY SISTERS
ARE NOT WITHOUT THEIR REASONS—for selling out that is.

As a child I thought I'd like to live
On the Côte d'Azur,
Which I imagined to be blue-lit, pale and empty,
bare white rocks

and palm trees under a ferocious uncolored sun.
I thought Robinson Crusoe
lived on the Côte d'Azur with his faithful Friday.

And Mother sang in the bath—suicide songs,
Father called them.

•   •   •

We drank Sanka out on the screened porch
and listened to the owls calling from the empty lot next door.
Grandfather wanted Uncle Peedee to build on that lot,
but he wouldn't. He bought a house down the street
and lived there with his wife, Maude the Electrified Woman.
She was old, Maude, she had hair the color of smoke and twitched.

I am divided against myself, mean sometimes,
but I have decided *I am not a mean person*. My wife
was mean—I said that to the judge. Oh sure, he said,
and snickered. My father's last years
were spent quietly, reading Proust. He'd glance up
from time to time—a look of torment in his face.
You'd wait for that, for the sad, ugly expression
of regret tinged with shame and fury, and we grew
to hate it. We wrote about it in our diaries.
Three sisters and a brother locked into our rooms
scribbling.

•   •   •

Dear Diary : Today I caught a dose of father's "Look"
and wanted to kill him. Am I crazy?

The Monkey Woman—that's what my sisters
called my wife. They could be cruel, my sisters,

but they had no power. "We live in South Georgia,"
Arlene wrote, "at one with the bugs and the snakes."
Now they never leave the house.

I was small for my age. They say you never get
over something like that, but I think I have.
As an adult I'm a little short,
but not too much. If I was a dwarf I think it
would be worse. "You get a woman to love you,"
my uncle said, "you'll be okay." His squinty wife
Maude peered down at me from her
Electrified distance, head crackling with static.

My grandmother could picture anyone naked.

•   •   •

And sometimes I think the sunset
hates the darkening houses.

When the robbers made Father take his clothes off
and kneel before them I wished I could have fainted.
I see the vanes of my mother's tragic face
behind the rain, all that,
which I have explained to you in my letter
and would like to spend an evening talking about, if you'd let me.
Please respond to this note posthaste.

Dusk, Like the Messiah

For Michael Block

Dusk, like the Messiah, appears everywhere all at once while we are thinking
how love never really lets up and everyone,
so we've come to realize, is innocent of his crimes,
just as they told us—the little talkers and
spokesmen out in the daylight, the ravers and constant jokers who
never get anywhere (they mentioned this)—and once again a surprising
and unencumbered tenderness seeps into crevices and conversations where
    the one speaking,
for just a second, looks up from the discourse and goes quiet as if he gets it.

from WORD COMIX

I Speak to Fewer People

I have been in touch lately with my inner self,
the fruit picker who lived all those years in a motel.
I shaded my story so it proved everything I did was
by intention. After each love affair, each participant
received a little gift. I mean someone always said:
You didn't really love her. I speak to fewer people
than ever. No matter what it looks like—I say this
every chance I get—something divine is going on.
And wonder: Is it? I'd like to lose a little weight.
Just the same, the marriage had its good points.
I still can't tell you what I am known for. I'm easily
shamed. On my walks I hope to meet someone interesting,
someone I have been headed toward all my life,
or simply someone without too much guile, a friendly
person with a little intelligence. Maybe we will
walk along together, talking about romance or trucks.

Evasive Action

. . . the clipped possessive moment, the barber on his porch
cutting his son's hair, who looks for a second straight into the sun
and then back at his son's head now a golden, nodulous remnant,
a flower if he likes or Lenin's bumpy skull, he puts his scissors down
and goes inside and apologizes to his wife, who doesn't understand,
but who accepts his words like a private harvest she's storing up,
and then the son, who's going into the army, comes in, half cut,
and sees them and thinks he understands years of bickering,
but doesn't, and goes on to the battlefield where he writes his sister
saying we are not far from the truth of things, watching beyond his hand
two scorpions pick at each other, and thinks of days by the river, of his
father recovering from cancer, singing a song his grandmother memorized in Vienna
and his father, who hated his own mother, cursing her, revoking the song,
and the next moment he's blown apart and then sent home in a metal coffin
and the parents and the sister get up early on the day of his funeral
and eat breakfast silently on the porch, and this is going on barber after barber.

Abuses in the Big Hotels

Small birds, damaged by shellfire, slant against the light.
"The descent of wisdom . . ." the dictator begins,
and pauses, recalling his mother's wine-reddened face.
A residue of depression become ill will, a sensation
of engorgement, and an undeveloped moment in which the spirit stalls,
falls back and drops to its knees nervously trembling,
swing by. The old Cuban woman in the artist's photographs
seems less sinister today. Not long after midnight
sounds near the library like gunshots. The public yearns
for happiness, for exhilaration, instruction and seamless joy.
A frame-up fails. Light pours imprecisely over white coffins
tipped on their sides. An officer taking apart a man's face
regrets his lack of schooling. Acquaintances, called by the police,
resentfully clean the victim's apartment. A child is helplessly considerate,
misses what was said, wanders out of the backyard and disappears.
Grace naps in an empty garage. An illusion,
mistook for happiness, fades one afternoon about four.
The old man they watched six years straight do nothing yet
died between shifts. He left a bloody shirt once, in Tenerife,
and never went back for it. "I loved," the dictator says,
"the way my mother's body moved when she strolled along
holding herself in her arms. I have always loved
the elegant sway, the curve like infinity's cul de sac,
the seductive and unappeasable . . ." and stops talking.

One Lie After Another

I'd come so far, the last leg
in a shiny new car and then the ride on the special train

for the privileged & successful. A pigeon or a parrot
dressed up as a hawk with my fake beak

and tie-on sweptbacks and all. Then some brainiac
getting into the limo ahead of you, tossing

off a quip or saintly expression, something you never
expected: you stumble and glance up at the huge white buildings,

abruptly overcome. Why'd you even start?
You used to go around asking them how they did it.

How'd you get the motor going? What was it
you believed in? My buddy's a war correspondent now.

We lost touch after going sour in a poker game.
My ex-wife runs a store. Blah blah blah she used to say

when I tried to explain. Or *Help me help me.*

Evergreens

The year I admitted I was lonely
I didn't know what I was saying
      I said the nights are rough here
they have minikins & clowns
old postulates
taking out the trash and you
      get lonely sometimes. I didn't know
how one thing leads to another
like a smell under the house
      and then you're talking about the payoff
when you don't even want to
you want them to listen
like people with taps on their shoes
      who later as they heavily, roguishly dance,
think well of you.

The Paris of Stories

A specific passage in which the hero, painted blue,
howls in southern trees, that is, southern

France, and somebody says the City of Light
is this way, but you get close and it's getting darker along

the woody banks where statice and columbine
figure in a tale the apostle

of rationalism is telling to the converts,
who say this all happened before,

but then the apparent elaboration—the sunset, we mean—
striped like a figure of ridicule,

but brilliant, fucking sublime, the desperation turning to quality yellow
on our faces, the way

earth time includes these confusing generous passages,
gets to us, or to the one operating the ferry,

who leans back and lets his knotty fingers
trail in the water, thinking of his little life, so sweet to him.

Hollyhocks

. . . rosettes, or like those figs packed in a wheel:
hollyhock blooms stripped back to seed cases, summerworn capsules like tires
racked at a Gulf station in the dusty West of movies,
                    the stems of these flowers known in roadside
Navaho gardens rubbed raw, frayed, strips of pale plant matter
hanging from them like Brian Donlevy's

collar shreds
(in *The Glass Key*)
as he dresses to do the worst
to get the best (time
            stuttering, smirking
its way out of the area, slithering), the stringy bits of coating

stripped from the peduncle,
                    the tall skinny (stringbean) hollyhocks, and the
blooms *not like*
collar parts, or maybe studs (a spiky inflorescence),
rosaceous,
and Donlevy, like all of us,

secretly a hero, rugged
and noisy,
            filled with the lively force and animal good spirits
(Alan Ladd
his great fixer says, *He's on the dead up & up*)
            not always sufficient—I guess—

to keep us alive long enough
to bloom & proliferate, but must perish—we've agreed—

so it's not even a race, but only
a flowering, that fades—*one*

after the other—leaving seed satchels,
wreaths, discs, coronals, festoons, chaplets & annulations,
not raiment, a springboard or destiny, but like those columnar starter lights
at drag races, flashing on in June,

                    signaling summer's all clear,
the flowers tissuey yet slightly reptilian, *sostenuto*,
not spiraling, but set at intervals along the spike that's tough
and straight, the whole
shebang a fresh seeding
like a broken marriage you get up out of

and build a new life from, the attempt
to stay clear of what nearly killed you,
                    like one gazing
at a dusty desert landscape
                        who sees hollyhocks
blooming in the old woman's garden

next door—signals they look like—the garden tipped,
spun around like someone hit by a car
thrown down busted in a ditch
            and left there, torn, little brilliant lights
and important points of elegance & forthrightness
done in, flowers

like the shed skins of small gods or Bikini Atoll
shambling back,
        those bushes
with their internal gizmos and genetic structures rattled
dazed and pummeled near to shit,
                    maimed, little

Krazimotos, Igors, Ratzos
            and amiable mental midgets putting
forth a curtailed, counter radiance (like everybody), freakish,

like Alan
Ladd (imagination
& delicacy around the mouth, his
inability to miss
          what's really going on) revivifying
after William Bendix

beats his soul nearly out of his body,
the frayed
          and dying hollyhocks,
and the whole upended affair—
pattern scrambled—including the old lady's nondescript dog,
that, slowly,

like an aged *fabricateur* forgetting where he is,
                    or not caring anymore,
Samuel Beckett (*por ejemplo*) in the nursing
home
glancing up from a last piece of work,
starting to forget

          the intolerable situation—turns his big head, the dog,
among the broken stems of great flowers—kings,

queens
mit regalia—
garden worn to the nap,
          the underdebris, (shredded, dry) like a bed now—
turns his head and—unable
to comprehend the works of humankind—looks at you (so you say—*we say we say*),
          tenderly.

Like Odysseus, Like Achilles

Homer sleeping on the ground,
little rock angle if he's lucky, goatskin
tarp, he's headed to some nobleman's

house for Thanksgiving, it's late in the season,
Homer's wondering
why at his age he's still thinking of women, doxies

he calls them, heartless charmers, he wants
to get up and pace,
but the boy's fast asleep, and truth is,

he knows it's not the girls,
it's him, his craving, these broads,
he can't shake the habit, the loneliness

and the harsh poetry of life are simply too much
w/out chicks in it, the disconsolation, you
name it: troglodytic personal ghettoism,

godforsaken secludinous isolato apartheid,
Maraboutian pillarist enmonkment & eremitistic adytum,
he could go on and on, but he never does,

he's just a country boy, simple and straightforward,
his heart like a used-up farmer
in a bad crop year, longing for a life at sea.

Little Swan Songs Being Sung All Down the Block

Consider the good-byes you'd say to a baby in a satchel (*I got*
to get going now) the firebreaks broken through just in time
and the snarling child overrun by shame the unrestrictible
beauty of whole countries. Consider the rapidity
with which the world gets back to us the remarkably
festive nature of bridges in general. Consider how pigeon shadows
like black tears fall down the side of the Hotel W as you
grow more distant from possibility that is to say
are still on the killer's list. Consider please the
disputes settled by a glance the runaround still possible
mostly rescinded. Consider the refusal to let you in
the blasted heaths of love postmortems taking place in parking lots
and the rear projections of those—by themselves—falsely accused.
Consider the established way of speaking the unverifiable
particularities alluded to by a series of contestable affidavits
and a spiffy gent just cutting his eyes away. Consider
how dear the old man's look just was the subtlety uncapturable really
except if then in the royal flush of words if you were there to see it
the (consider this) still upright
moment beckoning like a tempestuous new lover just starting the tally.

Illustrated Guide to Familiar American Trees

I don't get it about the natural world.
Like, greenery,
without people in it, is supposed to do what?

City sunlight, I say, how can you beat it—
the walk to the pool after work, shine
caught in the shopkeeper's visor, bursts.

I see myself moving around New York,
snapping my fingers, eating fries.

My ex-wife's out in California.

I wish she was over on Bank Street,
up on the second floor,
and I was on the way there
to call to her from the sidewalk.

There's a cypress on that block, two honey
locusts and an oak. I love those trees
like my own brothers.

An Orange Light in the Windows

. . . of course there are cranberry bogs for sale
and rich partial distractions
you experience when a neighbor's carried off,
poisoned by his wife. You say we all deserve it

or wash the windows and sit in the truck listening
to Crawdaddy sing his blues,
but the interference you sense, the dusty needle points
and delays in your release date

are real, as real as anything is. Where will it come from
this time? Your check's
lost like an expedition to discover
the source of the Nile. Speculation used to be fun,

but you're overextended, gripped
by nervousness now.
The rainout lasted for weeks.
And then an infestation of varmints,

something disassociated from itself, from the crew,
and things were hazy
and tasted of flavored salt.
Where did you put

the thingamajig that was going to save you?
A disputed set of values
didn't look right.
What did she mean, about the smell?

Arthritis

. . . slow hitch and up pull of the hip,
the swing, knee barely flexing, the curve like

a sabal frond bent suddenly by wind, the foot flashing,
in a sense, forward, extended like the hood of a Bonneville, turned

slightly outward to catch with the face of the foot
the breeze, the Large Magellanic Cloud, to balance all there an instant,

the body upwardly following, appended, rising from the side
of itself like an architectural folly

or former city of light rising
from the excavated marl, the barely covered bones

aching all night, radiant like beacons
of a slow decay continuously occurring near us in the woods

out behind the mall, where boys with nothing else to do
run wild on Sundays, bellowing

and lashing each other with bicycle chains.

Out of the Way Bungalow-Style Areas

Sometimes love's vagrancy (whatever you call it)
overwhelms all but the most robust subscribers
and dishonest as it may sound the whole cramped enterprise
is given only a few minutes to clear out of town.

We were touchy that year, all year,
at least until the old lady died. Perhaps a singularity
enraptured you, caused the sell-off
and the false positive. Compare your notes

with the sample addresses, the ones
the boss started to give, but then just couldn't.
Outside the metropolis
you hardly find any restaurants worth eating in. Yet

the places are always full. Little families, conversation groups,
a sense of the fell and distracted nature of humankind,
the displaced circular reasoning one gets into after a gambling loss,
these show up, disperse among the tables

and fade into the background.
It appears we'll be here just long enough. For whatever
the thing is that knows no human reason to have its say. Or something
other, she explained, and passed the biscuits around.

As It Happened

Out in the snow
in bare places, windswept
behind filling stations in Vermont
on hillsides in the Maritime Provinces
by lakes where picnic benches
take up the thread of loneliness
the stillness behind
a remark recalled as one drives home
from the council meeting
the day
like an attempt to return
nonrefundable merchandise
dying in its own arms
the wind dying down
a softness in your wife's face
reminding you of something
you thought you'd never forget.

Summer in the Subtropics

I got interested in religion, licorice
and banana popsicles which signified the unusual
figurations of universal import, the carefully placed antecedents
and rabbity coverage we got in those days out in the sticks.
You get up and pray and
everything shelves away. The relatives smelling of swamp water
and licorice, the horses whinnying as if they mean it.
Then you try to believe what you're told. You get sores
in anterior cul de sacs. And after you finish the swimming lesson
they give you a popsicle. Does that explain it?
You think about her all day sometimes,
or like the time you said you didn't sleep
for fifty days, it seems like that. And now the arrangements
are going sour. They gather for their reunions—
we were never that close. And often from the background
made animal noises. Friendly animals, a little lost,
who might be coaxed out with a treat, at least at first.

Lariats

I suppose I want forgiveness for lying so bluntly
and not getting around behind the house
where the real work is, and I guess
I never got used to the suppositions
and colorful descriptions of harmonious doings
at the cotton gin or ancient château become a famous hotel.

The designs I had of random placement, of particular amenities,
passed with the night. I go where the fruit cups are.

Now the descriptions I read in the paper
of souls caught thieving, caught lying
about the body, always fit, always ring true.

I bought a car in Alabama
and drove it to Texas, traded it for a horse
and crossed into Mexico where I got arrested and sent back in a van
to Brownsville, put in a dormitory-style jail
and, after roughing up by agencies unleavened by courtesy, got out
on a hot dawn and sat in a cafe eating hominy soup,
thinking of Kafka and Henry Miller who
in his great books never mentioned visiting churches or the Louvre,
and wondered how my horse was, an ignoble, bitter animal I disliked.

Oh Yeah

Afterward my friend explains
how awkward it is for him when there's no set procedure
and like a country maddened by grief
where the populace runs shrieking into the jungle
he is forced to make conversation
with some man he has no control of, like the time in New Orleans
when his wife rolled the Mercedes and showed up
with half her hair burned off cursing the police,
or he was just standing there, he said, like a god, *Christ
you should've seen me*, and this nut started talking about
his farm in Mexico, and suddenly my friend sensed
no one knew anything, really, about how to keep loving
anyone, anyone at all,
and that's how you get off on these little fishing trips
where you lie in the tent by yourself reading
the journals of lost explorers, and without looking
you can sense the sun, the spectacular evaporate,
erasing everything, that's how you take it, personally,
as if a secret shelter is slowly being exposed to scrutiny
or the joke's starting to make sense.

About This Far

Still an unsolid customer,
piddler, careless among
sassafras, lupine
and other ditch life on summer days
I set my bare feet among
to let the progesteronic heat
swallow my mind
as the sun itself etc in this preview
or what is it I am saying
will someday
those others to come in their turn
as when the speedy car
veers and goes
out of control, whipping us
into eternity where ox-eye daisies
and blue asters burn.

Meaty Chunks

If I ask forgiveness will the sweetgum tree
bend down to me, or cherries fall in my lap,
or the substitute driver,
the one who never liked us, will he honk compunctiously—
a man troubled in sleep by furious agents
of change—become like us
in a knowledgeable way? Will I become the one
who on the group campout makes potato pancakes
and later walks by the lake fretting about Mother,
dying of a tumor in Portland? *Where to?* ask
the oversubscribed,
turning for direction to self-published maps
scribbled over with rage.
The pride I thought so much of
has, if not abated, turned into a sleeping pill.
I gain through decrease,
like a goalie. And sit in my car eating raspberry glacé,
waiting for the singalong to begin. The top of something
wants to come off, but still
I back away, like a trainee before a bear with its head
in a bucket. Ludicrous, I think, sweating
and scared, ordered to continue with whatever it was I just forgot.

Leaves in the Subway

Breeze stirred by a train's
arrival lifts a green, yellow and pale red maple leaf,
spins and tosses it onto a bench where a woman in
dark blue like an old-fashioned governess moves down a bit to give it room.

The subtlety of forgiveness is more important and the twice-told
matter of a young girl's triumph in her software class,
stays with us longer, I suppose, and then we have the carefully
placed moments in which one who has made trouble all along,
in an unfashionable flourish
and a prank conceived out of a need to quell loneliness,
attempts to catch the attention of those in the know, and fails.

I've given religion much thought and now sometimes attend services.
I don't suppose it'll hurt, unless I meet
a malefic individual who gains influence and makes me
do illegal things. But this probably won't happen. I got caught
a few years ago in an internet scam, and
spent several months
retrieving my identity, but for a while now
I've been untouched by crime. The days mount like saucers on a table.
I give to charity when I think of it and try not to dwell
on where the money really goes; being kind is the idea, after all.

Yesterday I drove to the mall and walked around.
The young pear trees were just transferring their business to fall.
They looked nifty and neat, not too tall and free of messy fruit.
I thought of Stendhal in his late years, still working,
without much success, and of Follain and his penetrating
sight, young girls climbing French hills
to their big or little deaths, never having
indicated much or spoken. My wife and I are planning
a move to France. It'll be fun. Next week we'll visit the embassy

to chat about expectations and services. Out my window fall's
piecing things together, sweeping up
and generally preparing the park for winter. Soon we'll be sledding
on the white Paris hills. I have a new snowsuit and boots
and can't wait to try them out. It's another way of making friends.

Extremadura

I'm tired, spent really,
but don't say much, lean toward the rookeries, spirulina
days, effect trooperish refrains, undeliquent and pressed,
not hardy but persistent still, in a fading way,
feel dunked-on, put-upon, dry-hearted often
in face of grief, bear trouble poorly, issue bulletins
to the Dept of the Interior
requesting stays and clarifications, sent to former
addresses. Querulous, taking too long to pee,
drafty, windy I mean, poised, or stuck, interested
in repellents,
chromium cures, provisional governments that stay on
forgetfully, crudely demanding
and ineffectual in a familiar way. Partial caps, vein splices,
unilateralisms, useful tips. Enormity
breaks through. The striation, evisceration of sunrise, dampened yellows
and parlous, disintegrating reds,
speedy particles stream, gravity, unspent grief, quivers at the fascia,
life a nolo contendere thing,
distent, then deflated, gurgling; raw winter fields,
boys kicking a football, a grainy, bottom-heavy mist almost too much
to bear, numb arguments pressed locally and taken
for universal truths, the next geezer over complaining,
or was that me, pushing at the fence that sags with our weight, and holds.

Chalk Pictures

Better, in the moment of application
when the fireball of impropriety or
failed deliverance, the inexcusable
act or defiance, the probative issue
related to the low-lit devilment dished
up by the local chapter, the pump
action love and refusal to commit
to a variance in affection, all these
stipulations and communards in their
best clothes standing by fire trucks
whistling light airs, to get going, better
to push right through the elemental
aspects, the universal complications
and hazardous cargo, apply a little
backyard chiffonade, minus lies,
forgo the shifts and decelerations,
and as the sun turns the moon to blue
sky, and birds sing, admit everything.

Pied Noir

At four I was put into steel-ribbed jackboots
in an attempt to shore up my ankles that they
said were too weak to hold me up on their own,
implausible, incomplete, half-wit mélanges,
frappés of bone and sinew, strapped into the
heavy oil-reeking burrow-like ordinance of my
black storm trooper boots that took twenty
minutes and all my tottish gifts to lace
up. I already knew how to read, having taught
myself by religiously studying the *Pogo* comic
books (Walt Kelly, artist) and so I knew from
the instructions, purpose and disclaimers
that accompanied the boots that these infernal
contraptions were designed to put the afflicted
child on equal footing with his peers. Equal
footing! Only if other children's feet were
set in cement. At once I knew that these clod
stompers were only another contrivance
conjured by my father to facilitate his task
of getting rid of me. Maybe he thought wearing
them would drive me to suicide—a laughingstock,
a humiliated person—or cause me to stumble
into traffic or provoke bullies to the point
that they would beat my head in with my
own steel-capped shoes. Nearly weeping,
grimacing with shame and unable entirely to
suppress his derisive laughter, Pop watched
with pornographic glee in his eyes as I laced
the leather pachyderms up. My choked-down
tears stung in my throat like Red Devil hot
sauce. In the backyard my mother shrieked
negatively, spewing her addled jazz. The
truth was I believed them. I accepted that

I was deformed, a local mutant who couldn't
walk straight or well. As I had raced barefoot
across lawns or dangled my feet in the
runoff creek I felt no pain or awkwardness.
But something must be wrong; they said so—
something invisible, something powerful
like the work of God, and it had warped
my toes and bent my ankles and stripped my
metatarsals of their power. At the same
time something else, a trashy, renegade
voice, only a tendency, a leniency, a notion,
rose in me. It rejected all the above
and suggested I was in the hands of killers.

The Greeks

I've been depressed lately about my general lack of advancement,
maybe that's it, nothing's coming out right,
and I thought man this is like a Greek tragedy,
but I read a book that said such business wasn't even ironic
and in most cases expected. I dream sometimes of going away,
but not as often as I used to, I've already cut out
so many times, started over, I don't know where I'd go
or don't trust—something, I stay where I am.
At the coffee bar where I go at daylight to work things through
a woman in straitlaced clothes comes in and goes out
nervously, asks for coffee, picks at her cuticles as she waits
looking around—I notice this
but it's as far as I go, the rounded cheeks, flat black eyes,
yes they're in there too, but no further than this, I don't speculate
for example about what she's doing. I'm growing more numb as time
passes except for the moment when the person next to me is spoken to
and I become acutely embarrassed, like an adolescent who's sure
everyone can see through to his mucky shame. I see many others
who're weary and nervous and sore of heart,
but you can't speak to them in a city like this
without taking a chance on getting battered. Best to save
your tender feelings for the totally bamboozled, the foot-dragging
crumpled homeless guy who pulls himself hand over hand through the subway car
bleating and holding out his wrinkled paper cup. He's like us, metaphorically,
a man with work to do, getting on with it, some slaphappy liberator
God's taken up on the mountain and beat the shit out of
and sent back down sans a tablet of laws or any instructions whatsoever.
Now he's here, dopey and persistent, we know the story, we're part of it,
a bunch of Greeks the gods have turned their faces from,
we're down here on the grimy beach arguing and ruining everything,
getting up each day like men getting out of garbage bags behind the 7-Eleven,
hoping some beauty's beckoning, some version, unstable but plucky,
something safe and new, might show up. By now I've encountered

a thousand ways of looking at life, read books about it,
yet still I like to venture out at dawn
which even as it begins is ending, gray streets slumped
in fog. Sometimes I catch sight of a fresh compilation.
It's a variable, meaning. Then I notice in her old driver's license photo
the sadness in my ex-wife's face; it was there all the time.
She's out of the picture now, you might say,
off plumbing the atribilious instant out in L.A. I remember waking up
after midnight thinking she's such a Nazi about the damn covers.
Wanting out, going into the bathroom to argue with myself,
nearly stupefied with regret that I'd ever married her.
Yet when it ended I cried for months. Is this Greek?
I don't know, human maybe. Everything's more tangled than ever.
Just now I'm thinking of old drunks, how their faces look doubled in size,
or the head shrunk, the skull back of the eyes,
brows tufty and separated by deep lines,
mouth slightly agape, lips slathered with a
purpose that's nearly faded out, the space between them shadowy
as if they've taken a small bite out of the dark
and hold it in their mouths, waiting for a drink to wash it down.
I'm minutes away from something important,
yet I don't know if I'll recognize it when it gets here.
Philoctetes, somebody, I think of him,
the wound that never heals, *there's* a story I could go for,
the slow stump up the beach towards the truth, or
maybe only the facts, some horrible revelation only minutes away.
Maybe stop for a donut or something, Phil, notice the pattern
if you can call it that, the windy momentum in the trees.

The Fall Schedule

The magisterial aspects of what's
left over are actually not enough
to foster the big-time proposals
you're looking for. A tent, white, filled
with musicians: that's what they
had in mind after the power failure. Love's,
that is. Foursquare and some episodes of
internal bleeding ago, we were almost
on top of things. The trees saw all
this in the way trees do, without saying
much. You got a light? I sat down
in the foyer like a protester, love's
strikeout artist, and decided to
devote myself to complicated matters.
The heat you feel's just the bodies
rotting underground. I thought that
up in the subway where once again
Car Seven was without a comeback.
You saw her calling for takeout,
but you didn't catch her name. I
mentioned this to the investigating
officers, but they were too exhausted
to pay attention. We'll get him
this time, they said, waving me away.
I thought I'd better go to Italy
or some place with old mismanaged fields
and sacks of potatoes stacked in
a barn by the woods where foxes
come out at night to romp in the grass.

The Adepts

The new day tunnels away under the oaks
and we see this,
see the shabby character and his religious radio,
the orthodox set of clouds above the park.
A few hang around speculating, getting over the night.
The rest are down on their knees praying
for forgiveness or for the triumph of their plans.
We're in tight with the dawn,
completely blown inside out, prostrate on the grass;
our shirts are burnt offerings,
our pants are carpets the priests walk on,
our bodies the sacrifice.

—Please accept my night in jail, my hangdog expression,
          the time I slept with my brother's wife;
please accept my desperate connivance, my
          loss of respect, the way I carried
three oranges in a sack until they rotted—

All around us the monks
and priests, the nuns of fun
go on with morning prayers.
A sister with a speckled face
scoops holy water from the fountain
and sprinkles it over our bent backs,
caws like a crow and offers
her body to the assistant
priest who is busy counting the take.

—Please accept my unhappy belly,
          my yellow toes; please accept
my cynical eyeballs and my variations on the theme
          of destitution; please accept
the nothing I am and the nothing I shall become—

There's a bustle in the oaks,
a stir in the maple trees;
the wind picks up. Jesus,
in the shape of a juicer,
gets out of the busted limo on the corner.
He hands out donuts,
steps into the bushes to pee.
God is the dog smell in his clothes,
the furtive look,
the broken fingers on his right hand,
the dirt filling in the lines on his palm.
God is the remains of memory
and the disconsolate muttering,
the braggadocio on the corner
who's as untrustworthy as he looks.
—it's a sunlit fruit peel, constant
reminders from the police,
the favoritism of certain officials,
dampened bread, the wet construction site
of her mouth, it's the fat
transvestite at the spigot
undressing down to her manhood
shaved pink as a baby's,
and the one-legged pigeon Mother Superior
chases with a broken umbrella.

—Please accept my lack of belief,
*   my war with decomposition;*
please accept my utter disregard
*   for the ornamental*
arrangements, the displaced,
*   overlooked and sometimes eerily*
unavailable
*   creed we all live by,*
the scrap upon which is written
*   the one true word—*

Whatever you have,
says the peculiar and dusty God,
I want that.

Unburnt Offerings

Day knocks back in yellows and bright
levantine blues, thin shades of a color lost to the Mayans,
rediscovered over St Pete around six. Vacations

rescinded, interrupted by a solemn episode, a few words at a grave.
Carefully, with no intent
to harm, two brothers break into the back of Saul's Electrical Supply,

looking for gimmicks. Friends of a lifetime wake
separately in unfamiliar beds, choking on guilt. *Reconciliation
comes too soon*, a woman thinks, and turns back to her dream.

A famous toastmaster, eating from a sack of *churros*,
decides to leave his wife for the love of a good man. The mayor
checks his bulldog's teeth. *Pain's my name,*

the ER doctor says, *or, no—my game*, he says—*oh gosh*,
and falls off the toilet with a heart attack. *Infarction*, his six-year-old whispers
as he takes out the garbage, and looks up at the sky where something

heretofore impossible to get a handle on seems to be separating itself from the casual run of
clouds.
Grapefruit pulp coats the back wheels of a delivery truck on Stock Street.

A young man attempting to memorize
a paragraph from the *Call & Appeal* recalls what
he meant to say at the confab, a quote from

Francis Bacon concerning the indefatigability of—*what was it?* A policeman,
fossicking his wife's vagina, decides to come clean. *Sweetness,*
the child model thinks, *that's what keeps me going. Or do I mean* tendresse?

Clean

Flattened, sprawled out, snuffling like a dog,
I sniff the expectorate and the feculent lost phenomena,
the shavings and culls, the drifted apart discards
and answers become complications heaved into the grass.
I slide on my belly over the damp places
where old men lay down to try the earth on for size.
In misused areaways behind buildings, among the grassy footings
and slippery spots where disgusting practices ended up, I find
a kind of happiness. My body's covered with what's down there.
Mottled and stained, I've become one with the particulate, the crumb,
the soiled and ineradicable section, the sulcated and unattended spot.
I follow the hog trail of longing. The lowdown is my fortune.
The fundament, the footing, the radicle, the rhizoid, the parquet.
Mouth stuffed with dirt, I chew the bulletins of governance and desire
and take comfort in the filth, in the place
of failure and exudation. I am at home among fistulas
and burned patches, down there with the stems, the shrieks that failed
to arouse pity, the exogenous hopes tossed out with the trash.
What I gather about me was there before I came.
It is often slick and pulpy like a mango,
hot like the scrap of cat hide the sun shines on,
and in its capacity to represent the likelihood of a life beyond
integrity and consummation, I am solaced.
I make small flapping motions, I scurry
my feet and spirate, dragging myself forward,
paying a manifest attention to the tiny voices of ant wings and drying spittle,
and I repeat what they say. In the faint resettlings
of dust and endlessly reducible fractions
I recognize my own voice. Like them I am not saying anything important.
Like them—like the torn-off bee abdomens and locust petals,
the crusts—I have left behind the designs
and purposes I was built for. I am free to inch along,
without meaning. Among the lost

I'm found. I present to myself the unoccupied remainders and
disarranged failed circumstances, the painted tin receptacles
and scuffed flooring of transience: among the discarded, discarded:
among the deserted, the marooned, the forsook, I am part of things.
Now the casual elimination is acceptable to me,
the object hurled down in fury or bitterly tossed aside,
the letter torn to pieces,
the wedding ring in feckless ceremony placed
between two slightly larger stones and covered with moss,
the torn-away excess
and deliveries that failed to reach their destinations—
all are acceptable, as are the messy discharges and the exuviation.
Relinquishments, the scattering of pieces, erasures and jettisons,
the fatally incomplete, are equal in my sight.
I flutter and scramble, I drag myself overhand,
leaving a trail, abreast of the trash,
keeping up with dereliction, equal with the failed repairs,
the designs growing more marginal as we speak.
It is here I find the endings that in their perfections of absolute loss
have become beginnings again, the bitten-off phrases and
inconspicuous wadding of spoiled opportunity about to start over.
I see the lost revamped. The mortified recast.
The crapped-out recombined with the useless to make the futile.
All the old possibilities—corrigendious, bone-headed and radiant—are here.

Compensation

. . . tiptap slips, hammer blows, all obvious, no nonsense,
make-right work, boys go crazy . . . *You press her hard,* she says,
you can see her mind overheat, the madness flood her . . .
dreams of summer in midwinter Manhattan, trash spills
out bins, white streaks, boys sleep on salt piles,
no resistance after a while, we give in,
to loneliness, to pain, to the devil and indulgence,
all life a contortion pressed through a slot
in time, remnants fall, crumbs that become
ponds in city parks, trees stained gold by autumn sun, love's cha-cha-cha.

Index of Titles and First Lines